**● soho theatre**

Soho Theatre in association

MW00328921

# A Couple of Poor, Polish-Speaking Romanians

by Dorota Masłowska
translated by Lisa Goldman and Paul Sirett

First performed at Soho Theatre on 28 February 2008

www.PolishCulture.org.uk

Soho Theatre is supported by

  **Bloomberg**

Performances in the Lorenz Auditorium
Registered Charity No: 267234

# Writer's Foreword

I was 22 when it was proposed to me that I write something for the theatre, but my experience of reading and seeing plays has been not only unsuccessful, but infrequent, and altogether very unpromising. I began from the most surrealist ideas and characters with operetta and futuristic psychologies, but in order to finally write a play, I recreated almost moment by moment an episode of my life from that time, travelling in a car the length and breadth of Poland. At the time I wasn't especially happy and the only thing I remember was a display of petrol stations, disposable places, with plastic cutlery, condoms, false food from a microwave, where the feeling is of being no one and being nowhere, or rather a feeling of being anybody anywhere, and a feeling of being stripped of definition and mask that was realised with a unique sharpness. So Romania – in this play – is rather not a popular country in south-eastern Europe, but a state of social weightlessness, when suddenly all costumes, props, ideas, definitions and honorary decorations become unverified, and unimportant like tickets.

I know, more or less, what this play meant in Warsaw, I am very interested to find out what it will mean presented in multicultural London where the situation of disguising yourself as someone 'other' becomes the situation of disguising one 'other' as a different 'other'. When we were working on the English version of the play, I realised that the amount 'lost in translation' was not much bigger than that 'found in translation'.

Above all I got to know something about my identity, which is constituted on negation. Instead of saying 'I am this', you say 'I am not this, nor this, nor that'. You don't say 'I am a Pole' but 'I am definitely not a Czech and even more definitely not a German'. I will explore this subject further. In the meantime I've started multilayered socio-philosophical explanations about my own text, which is a situation as paranoid as it is embarrassing, so I will end now quickly before you start to think that *A Couple of Poor, Polish-Speaking Romanians* is simply a story about a boy and a girl, who didn't know what to do with their time or time didn't know what to do with them and the decision as to how it really was I will leave to the people who write press releases for newspapers handed out in the tube and others who like to make decisions like these.

**Dorota Masłowska**

# Translator's Introduction

We don't yet know how the most recent wave of Polish migrants will influence British culture, but we know from our experience of previous groups of migrants that their influence will be significant. We have all read about the boost to the Catholic church in the UK, but we hear less about the many Polish people more than happy to escape its claustrophobic influence. As with any culture, there is no homogeneity.

Dorota Masłowska exemplifies this. At 24 she is the *enfant terrible* of the Polish literary scene, speaking to a young generation who can't remember 'communism' but who are against capitalism in Poland, with its unemployment and social problems, its often right-wing church and government. *A Couple of Poor, Polish-Speaking Romanians* reflects these political themes but not in the sociological, literal way of much British theatre. At heart it is a deeply personal play about loneliness, about driving into oblivion.

One of the toughest provocations in the play is the use of the word Romanian. Like many of Dorota's provocations it is uncomfortable. Romanian gypsies arrived in Poland in the early '90s to experience a xenophobic backlash and Dorota's vivid memory of this informs the play, but the Romania that Dorota writes about here is not a literal Romania, it is a social-psychological state, a feeling of being outside the 'norm' of Polish society, of resisting it and being rejected by it.

As an intercultural city, London is very different to Warsaw and the resonance of otherness is also different. Yet resonances there are in the play. Linguistically the play is 'other too'. Dorota is an iconoclast, famous for taking liberties with the Polish language, playing word games and making deliberate 'mistakes' with grammar and structure and street slang. It was tough and exhilarating to translate this blunt, odd, otherness from Polish into English.

Our guiding principal in the translation process was Dorota's zany imagination, her love of nonsense, her dark, ironic take on everything. Sitting and laughing, in Warsaw and London, being creative with words together, in Polish and English slang, this was our way into her puns, rhymes, syntactical gymnastics, idiomatic inventiveness and vulgarity.

'No, not that way round, it's too normal'. Dorota would laugh as we sat discussing a more 'naturally' English way to translate something, then adding with a glint in her eye, 'I have destroyed Polish and now I destroy the English language too.' We have substituted UK slang and puns for Polish ones and made some up as Dorota did. We have translated characters as culturally Polish and linguistically English, we have not changed the setting and unless humour or sense dictated otherwise, we have retained Polish cultural references – for example Father Gzregorz from the TV series *Plebania*. We felt it was important for the first English language production of this influential young writer's only play, not to impose parallels or 'improvements' to the original.

We would like to thank Pawel Potorocyzn of the Polish Cultural Institute for connecting us with TR Warszawa, thanks to its Dramaturg Piotr Gruszczynski for introducing us to the play via Benjamin Paloff's American translation, to Agneskia Blonska for her assistance with the literal translation and of course to Dorota Masłowska herself for both writing and dissecting her play with us.

In seeking out Dorota Masłowska, in translating and producing *A Couple of Poor, Polish-Speaking Romanians*, we hope to engage an intercultural audience with cutting-edge new writing from Poland – work which might be provocative and intriguing to English speakers, English-speaking Poles, Polish-speaking Brits and maybe even Polish-speaking Romanians.

**Lisa Goldman and Paul Sirett, February 2008**

Soho Theatre in association with the Polish Cultural Institute presents the English language / UK premiere of

# A Couple of Poor, Polish-Speaking Romanians
by **Dorota Masłowska**
translated by **Lisa Goldman** and **Paul Sirett**

| | |
|---|---|
| Parcha | **Andrew Tiernan** |
| Dżina | **Andrea Riseborough** |
| Driver & Mr Wiesiek | **Howard Ward** |
| Bartender | **Valerie Lilley** |
| Woman Driver | **Ishia Bennison** |
| Old Man | **John Rogan** |
| | |
| Director | **Lisa Goldman** |
| Designer | **Miriam Buether** |
| Lighting Designer | **Jenny Kagan** |
| Sound Designer & Music | **Matt McKenzie** |
| Assistant Director | **Agnieszka Blonska** |
| Choreography | **Rosie Kay** |
| Production Manager | **Matt Noddings** |
| Stage Manager | **Dani Youngman** |
| | |
| Deputy Stage Manager | **Tamsin Palmer** |
| Assistant Stage Manager | **Fiona Coombe** |
| Wardrobe Supervisor | **Sophie Toulouze** |
| Casting | **Nadine Hoare** |

Soho Theatre would like to thank Monika Bobinska and Pawel Potoroczyn.

# Cast

**Andrew Tiernan**  *Parcha*

Theatre includes *Flesh Wound* (Royal Court / Galway Theatre), *True West* (Bristol Old Vic), *A Lie of the Mind, The Bullet* (Donmar Warehouse), *Noise* (Soho Theatre) and *The Dispute* (Azor).

Film includes *Stone's War, 300, Snuff-Movie, rehab, The Red Siren, The Pianist, Mr In-Between, The Bunker, The Criminal, Face, The Scarlet Tunic, Playing God, Small Time Obsession, Snow White in the Black Forest, Interview with a Vampire, Two Deaths, Being Human, The Trial, As You Like It* and *Edward II*.

Television includes *Spartacus, Midsomer Murders, Dalziel and Pascoe, Cold Blood, Waste of Shame, Spooks, Life on Mars, The Quatermass Experiment, Murphy's Law, The Rotter's Club, Whose Baby is it Anyway, Murder Investigation Team, Waking the Dead, Red Cap, William and Mary, McCready and Daughter, In a Land of Plenty, Jonathan Creek, Cracker* and *Prime Suspect*.

**Andrea Riseborough**  *Dżina*

Theatre includes *The Pain and the Itch* (Royal Court), *Miss Julie/Measure for Measure* (RSC & Theatre Royal Bath), *Burn/Chatroom/Citizenship* (National Theatre) and *A Brief History of Helen of Troy* (Soho Theatre).

Television includes *Being Human, The Long Walk to Finchley, Party Animals, Mrs Beeton, Doc Martin, A Very Social Secretary* and *Whatever Love Means*.

Film includes *Love You More, Mad Bad & Sad,* Mike Leigh's *Happy Go Lucky, Magicians* and *Venus*.

**Howard Ward**
*Driver & Mr Wiesiek*

Theatre includes *Warhorse, The Good Hope, The Mysteries, Johnny on the Spot, Wind in the Willows, Mountain Giants, Night of the Iguana* (National Theatre), *All's Well That Ends Well, As You Like It, The Balcony, Speculators* (RSC), *Heartbreak House, Neville's Island* (Watford Palace Theatre), *How Long is Never, Fabulation* (Tricycle Theatre), *Under the Black Flag, Coriolanus* (Globe Theatre), *The Prayer Room* (Birmingham Rep/Edinburgh Lyceum), *Incomplete and Random Acts of Kindness, Night Owls, A Day in Dull Armour, Faith, Pale Horse* (Royal Court), and *Six Degrees of Separation* (Royal Exchange, Manchester).

Television and film includes *Doctors, Casualty, The Broken, Cash Back, Ghost Squad, Heartbeat, The Government Inspector, Family Affairs, Absolute Power, Amnesia, Murder Investigation Team, Unconditional Love, The Bill, Holby City, Inspector Lynley Mysteries, Gypsy Girl, Burnside, This is Personal, Dream Team, Insiders, Eastenders, Jake's Progress, Peak Practice, Between the Lines* and *London's Burning*.

**Valerie Lilley**  *Bartender*

Theatre includes *Small Thing* (Paines Plough), *Midden, Madhouse in Goa* (Coliseum Theatre, Oldham), *Fen & Faraway, Jane Eyre* (Sheffield Crucible), *Loyal Women, Flying Blind* (Royal Court), *The True Life and Fiction of Mata Hari* (Watford Palace Theatre), *The Beauty Queen of Leenane* (Salisbury Playhouse), *On Raftery's Hill* (Druid Theatre Company/Royal Court), *Holy Mothers* (Ambassadors Theatre), *Blue Heart* (Royal Court and tour), *The Mai, A Love Song for Ulster, Factory Girls* (Tricycle Theatre), *Drive On* (Lyric Theatre, Belfast), *Pig's Ear* (Liverpool Playhouse Studio), *Lysistrata, Juno and the Paycock* (Contact Theatre, Manchester), *My Mother Said I Never Should, Blood Wedding, Some Kind of Hero* (Octagon Theatre, Bolton), *The Cherry Orchard, The Card, Once a Catholic* (New Victoria, Stoke), *Killing the Cat* (Soho Theatre/Royal Court), *Shadow of a Gunman, Skirmishes, Breezeblock Park, All My Sons* (Liverpool Playhouse), *Inventing a New Colour*

(Royal Court/Bristol Old Vic), *Soapbox* (Manchester Library), *On Yer Bike* (Belgrade, Coventry), *Kennedy's Children, Beggar's Opera, Flying Blind, Camino Real, Coming and Goings* (Liverpool Everyman), *John, Paul, George, Ringo and Bert* (West End), *The Plough and the Stars* (Nottingham Playhouse), *Ghosts, Hamlet* (Victoria, Stoke-on-Trent), and *Shadow of a Gunman* (Mermaid Theatre).

Television includes *The Catherine Tate Show, Doctors, The Commander, Courtroom, Messiah 3, Court Drama, Serious and Organised, Grange Hill, Crime and Punishment, Anybody's Nightmare, Inspector Linley, First Communion Day, Hope and Glory, Peak Practise, The Rag Nymph, Famous Five, Brookside, Missing Persons, Elidor, Blood on the Dole, The Riff Raff Element, Eastenders, Nice Town, Children of the North, The Bill, Loving Hazel, Minder, Brookside, The Refuge, Final Run, Albion Market, Night of a Campaign, Give Us a Break, The Long March, Scully* and *Coronation Street.*

Film includes *I Know You Know, Cheeky, Priest* and *Scrubbers.*

## Ishia Bennison  *Woman Driver*

Theatre includes *The Gunpowder Season, A New Way to Please You, Sejanus His Fall, Speaking Like Magpies, Cymbeline, Measure for Measure* (RSC), *Strange Orchestra, Once We Were Mothers, Mother Courage* (Orange Tree), *Who's Afraid of Virginia Woolf* (Manchester Library), *Arabian Nights* (Young Vic), *Antony and Cleopatra, A Midsummer Night's Dream, The Merry Wives of Windsor, Richard III, Poetry or Bust* (Northern Broadsides), *Medea* (Lilian Baylis), *Les Miserables, Red Devils* (Nottingham Playhouse), *Turcaret* (Gate Theatre), *One for the Road* (Meridian Productions) and *Educating Rita* (Oxford Playhouse).

Television includes *True Dare Kiss, At Home with the Braithwaites, Coronation Street, Burnside, Love Hurts, Give and Take, Mother's Day, Story Teller, Bread, Eastenders, Much Ado About Nothing, Mitch: A Family Affair, Kessler* and *Bid for Power.*

Film includes *King David, Anno Domini, The Awakening* and *Jesus of Nazareth.*

## John Rogan  *Old Man*

Theatre includes several seasons with the RSC, *Awake and Sing, Macbeth, The Iceman Cometh, The Saxon Shore* (Almeida), *Buried Child, The Playboy of the Western World, Peer Gynt, The Cripple of Inishmaan, The Machine Wreckers, Richard II* (National Theatre), *Jumpers* (National Theatre/West End/Brooks Atkinson Theatre, New York), *Things You Shouldn't Say Past Midnight* (Soho Theatre), *Plasticine* (Royal Court), *The Loves of Cass McGuire* (Druid Theatre Company), *Charley's Aunt* (Watford Palace Theatre), *Loot, Entertaining Mr Sloane* (Birmingham Rep), *On Borrowed Time* (Southwark Playhouse), *The Matchmaker* (Chichester Festival and tour), *La Bête, Public Enemy* (Lyric, Hammersmith), *Our Town* (Shaftesbury Theatre), *The Plough and the Stars* (Young Vic), *Into the Woods* (Phoenix Theatre), *London Assurance* (Haymarket Theatre), *Love's Labour's Lost, The Rivals, Reunion in Vienna* (Chichester Festival Theatre), *The Film Society, Observe the Sons of Ulster Marching Towards the Somme* (Hampstead Theatre), *All's Well That Ends Well* (Martin Beck Theatre, New York), *The Skin of our Teeth* (Royal Exchange, Manchester), *Happy End* (Oxford Playhouse) and *Born Yesterday* (Greenwich Theatre).

Television includes *The Bill, Holby City, Servants, Christopher Wren: Master of the Universe, Weirdsister College, Father Ted, Broken Glass, Demob, Woodcock, The Buddha of Suburbia, Making Out, Poirot, Boon, Small World, Porterhouse Blues* and *Squaring the Circle.*

Television films include *Dr Jekyll and Mr Hyde*, *Caleb Williams* and *Dangerous Davies*. Film includes *Lecture 21*, *Intermission*, *Doctor Sleep*, *Richard II*, *Drowning by Numbers*, *The Old Jest*, *Foreign Body*, *Caravaggio* and *Scum*.

# Company

## Dorota Masłowska  *Writer*

Dorota Masłowska was born July 3, 1983 in Wejherowo, and grew up there. She applied to the University of Gdańsk's faculty of Psychology and was accepted, but left her studies for Warsaw, where she joined the Culture Studies course at Warsaw University. She first appeared in the mass-media when her debut book *Wojna polsko-ruska pod flagą biało-czerwoną* (translated to English as either *White and Red* in the UK or *Snow White and Russian Red* in the US) was published. Largely controversial, mostly because of the language seen by many as vulgar, cynical and simple, the book was praised by many intellectuals as innovative and fresh. A notable example of post-modernist literature, her book became a best-seller in Poland and won Masłowska several notable awards as well as general support among the critics. It was almost immediately translated into several languages, including French, German, Spanish, Italian, Dutch, Russian, English, Hungarian and Czech. Her second book, a rap-poem entitled *Paw Królowej* (*The Queen's Peacock / The Queen's Puke*) won her the NIKE, the major Polish literary award, in 2006. Later that year, she wrote the play *A Couple of Poor, Polish-Speaking Romanians*, first performed in Warsaw in Autumn 2006 and still running. Besides the London performance, the play is going to be staged in German, at Berlin's Gorky Theatre in Spring 2008.

## Lisa Goldman  *Director/ Translator*

Lisa is the Artistic Director of Soho Theatre. *A Couple of Poor, Polish-Speaking Romanians* is her third show, following on from the success of *Baghdad Wedding* by Hassan Abdulrazzak (which she recently directed as a Radio 3 Sunday play) and *Leaves of Glass* by Philip Ridley. As founding Artistic Director of the Red Room, Lisa developed and directed a huge body of radical new writing over 10 years. Her production *Hoxton Story* was a site-specific walkabout piece, which she wrote and directed. Other recent new plays developed and directed include *The Bogus Woman* (Fringe First-Bush/Traverse/ tour/Radio 3 Sunday play), *Bites* (Bush Theatre) and *Animal* (Soho Theatre), *Hanging* (CBL Radio 4 Friday play) all by Kay Adshead, curating *Going Public* (Tricycle Theatre), *Playing Fields* by Neela Dolezalova (Soho Theatre Company), *Made in England* by Parv Bancil, *Sunspots, Know Your Rights* and *People on the River* all by Judy Upton. *Ex, Obsession and Surfing* (All Critics' Choice BAC) and a 35mm short film *My Sky is Big* (NFT 1 & festivals) all by Rob Young. Lisa's long term producing collaboration with Anthony Neilson has enabled the creation of some of his finest work – *The Censor, Stitching* (both Time Out Live Award winners) and *The Night Before Christmas*.

## Paul Sirett  *Translator*

Productions of Paul's plays include *The Big Life* (Theatre Royal Stratford East & West End), *Lush Life* (Live Theatre, Newcastle), *Rat Pack Confidential* (Nottingham Playhouse/Bolton Octagon & West End), *A Night In Tunisia, Worlds Apart, Crusade, Jamaica House* (all Theatre Royal Stratford East) and *Skaville* (Bedlam, Edinburgh & Soho Theatre). Radio plays include *Vissi D'Arte, Hellhound On My Trail* and

Eva Bergen (all BBC Radio 4). Awards include *Vissi D'Arte* (LBC/LAB New Radio Playwrights – Winner, New York Radio Festival – Best Play & Best Writer, Prix Italia – Special Commendation), *World Apart* (Thames Television Theatre Writers Scheme – Best Play), *Rat Pack Confidential* (City Life – Best production), *The Big Life* (Olivier Awards, Evening Standard, TMA Awards – nomination for Best Musical). Paul was Literary Manager at Soho Theatre from 1994 to 2001 and Dramaturg at the Royal Shakespeare Company from 2001 to 2005.

## Miriam Buether  *Designer*

Miriam trained in theatre design at Central Saint Martins and in costume design at Akademie für Kostüm Design in Hamburg. Design Credits for Theatre and Dance (set and costume) include *My Child* (Royal Court Theatre), *The Bacchae* (National Theatre of Scotland), *The Wonderful World of Dissocia* (Royal Court Theatre), *Sacrifice* (Welsh National Opera), *Generations* (Young Vic), *Realism* (National Theatre of Scotland), *Long Time Dead* (Theatre Royal Plymouth), *Trade* (RSC/Soho Theatre), *pool (no water)* (Frantic Assembly), *Unprotected* (Liverpool Everyman), *The Bee* (Soho Theatre, Tokyo), *The Death of Klinghoffer* (Edinburgh International Festival/Scottish Opera), *After the End* (Traverse Theatre), *Way to Heaven* (Royal Court Theatre), *Platform* (ICA), *Outsight* and *Tender Hooks* (Foundation Gulbenkian, Lisbon), *Guantanamo* (Tricycle Theatre/ West End/ NY), *Body Of Poetry* (Komische Opera, Berlin), *Hartstocht* (Introdans in The Netherlands), *Track* (Scottish Dance Theatre), *Red Demon* (Young Vic Theatre, Tokyo), *Bintou* (Arcola Theatre), *Possibly Six*, *Tenderhooks* (Canadian National Ballet), and *7DS* (Sadler's Wells). Awards include the 1999 Linbury Prize, 2004/5 Critics Award for Theatre in Scotland for *The*

*Wonderful World of Dissocia*, 2007 TMA Award nomination for *Long Time Dead*, 2007 Evening Standard Award nomination for *My Child*.

## Jenny Kagan  *Lighting Designer*

Jenny trained as an actress and worked as a stage manager before turning to lighting design. Previous productions directed by Lisa Goldman include lighting for: *Leaves of Glass* by Philip Ridley and *Baghdad Wedding* by Hassan Abdulrazzak, both for Soho Theatre; *Bites* by Kay Adshead at the Bush and collaborating on *Hoxton Story* for The Red Room. Other work includes: *Burial at Thebes*, Nottingham Playhouse and Barbican; the UK Tour of *Miss Saigon*; *Endgame* and *House on the Beach* for National Theatre of Wales; *L'Elisir d'Amore* for New Zealand Festival; USA Network's tour of *Oliver*; *Pan* at the Capitol Theatre in Sydney; *Sacred Ellington* at the Barbican performed by Jessye Norman; *Who's Afraid of Virginia Woolf* at the Almeida and Aldwych Theatres and *Hamlet*, Bristol Old Vic. Jenny has worked as Associate Lighting Designer with David Hersey over many years including the National Theatre and Broadway productions of *Oklahoma* and *My Fair Lady*, *Jesus Christ Superstar* and *Martin Guerre* in the West End and worldwide productions *of Les Miserables* and the Sam Mendes production of *Oliver!*

## Matt McKenzie  *Sound Designer & Music*

Matt McKenzie came to the UK from New Zealand in 1978. He toured with Paines Plough before joining the staff at The Lyric Theatre Hammersmith in 1979 where he designed the sound for several productions. Since joining Autograph in 1984, Matt has been responsible for the sound design for the opening of Soho Theatre along with its productions of *Baghdad Wedding, Leaves of Glass, Blue Eyes* and Heels, Badnuff; Vertigo (Guildford); Saturday, Sunday, Monday, Easy Virtue (Chichester); Frame 312 (Donmar Warehouse); Iron (The Traverse and Royal Court). In the West End, theatre credits include: Made in Bangkok, The House of Bernarda Alba, A Piece of My Mind, Journey's End, A Madhouse in Goa, Barnaby and the Old Boys, Irma Vep, Gasping, Map of the Heart, Tango Argentino, When She Danced, Misery, Murder is Easy, The Odd Couple, Pygmalion, Things we do for Love, Long Day's Journey into Night and Macbeth. For Sir Peter Hall credits include: Lysistrata, The Master Builder, School for Wives, Mind Millie for Me, A Streetcar Named Desire, Three of a Kind and Amaedeus (West End and Broadway). Matt was Sound Supervisor for the Peter Hall Season (Old Vic and The Piccadilly) and designed the sound for Waste, Cloud 9, The Seagull, The Provok'd Wife, King Lear, The Misanthrope, Major Barbara, Filumena and Kafka's Dick. Work for the RSC includes: Family Reunion, Henry V, The Duchess of Malfi, Hamlet, The Lieutenant of Inishmore, Julius Caesar and Midsummer Night's Dream.

## Agnieszka Blonska
*Assistant Director*

Agnieszka trained at Bristol Old Vic Theatre School (Drama Directing, 2006-2007); School of Physical Theatre (London, 2003-2004); 'The Guildia Project' with New World Performance Laboratory (2000-2001) and The Academy of Theatre Practices, Gardzienice, Poland (1999-2001). She also completed an MA in Applied Social Sciences specialising in Anthropology of Culture, at Warsaw University, Poland.

In May 2007 she directed Philip Ridley's Vincent River at the Alma Theatre in Bristol (BOVTS diploma). Previously she directed A Pinch of Dandyism, scenes from The Bacchae by Euripides, scenes from After Liverpool by James Saunders, her own short

film Wind Up and the read-through of Escape by Adrian Harris for the South West Writers Group at the Bristol Old Vic. She has also assisted on various productions, including radio plays and television. In 2004 Agnieszka, together with Sean Palmer, formed the theatre company Equaldoubt' Since then the company has premiered four productions and one 'live installation'. They have toured the UK, Mexico, Slovakia and Poland. For the last three years Agnieszka has been collaborating with the street theatre company Desperate Men. In 2007 she also joined Wildworks Theatre on their wild adventures.

## Rosie Kay   *Choreographer*

Rosie trained at London Contemporary Dance School and, since graduating in 1998, has danced with various companies in the UK and Europe, set up her company Rosie Kay Dance Company in 2004 and has been awarded the Rayne Foundation Fellowship 2007. In January 2008 she was appointed an Associate Artist of DanceXchange, Birmingham. She was a soloist with Polish Dance Theatre, danced with Der Blaue Vogel in Berlin, Green Candle Dance Company and worked with choreographers Luca Silverstrini, Jonzi D, Jens Ostberg and Orian Anderson. Other work includes: Asylum and Other Stories (Touring & Dance Umbrella International Dance Festival). She has also worked in theatre (Birmingham Rep/ Young Vic/ Duckie at The Barbican), Opera (Opera Genesis, Royal Opera House 2) and Ballet (Mars, Ballet on the Buses; Birmingham Royal Ballet). Awards include: First Prize for Choreography at the International Solo Dance Theatre festival in 2000, the Bonnie Bird New UK Choreographers Award in 2003, shortlisted for the Samuel Beckett Theatre Award in 2004, Creative Class of Channel Four in 2005 and The Sunday Herald Award for Cultural Highlight of the Year 2006 for The Wild Party.

# ● soho theatre

- **Produces new work**
- **Discovers and nurtures new writers**
- **Targets and develops new audiences**

Under Artistic Director Lisa Goldman, Soho Theatre creates and enables daring and original new work that challenges the status quo by igniting the imaginations of writers, artists and audiences. We initiate new conversations with London and the wider world through projects that celebrate creative participation, internationalism and freedom of expression. We nurture a socially and culturally broad audience for theatre and create a buzz around theatre as a living and relevant art form.

*'a foundry for new talent... one of the country's leading producers of new writing'* (Evening Standard)

Soho Theatre has a unique Writers' Centre that offers an invaluable resource to emerging theatre writers. We are the nation's only unsolicited script-reading service that reports for free on over 2,000 plays per year.

Through the Verity Bargate Award, the Writers' Attachment Programme, and a host of development programmes and workshops we aim to develop groundbreaking writers and artists to broaden the definition of new theatre writing. Our learning and participation programme Soho Connect includes the innovative Under 11s scheme, the Young Writers' Group (18–25s), Script Slam and an annual site-specific theatre piece with the local community – most recently *Moonwalking in Chinatown*, in September 2007.

Alongside our theatre productions, Soho Theatre presents a high profile late-night programme with a mixture of groundbreaking comedy and performance from leading and emergent artists. We also curate a vibrant talks series and other events, encouraging the conversation to spill over into our new and reasonably priced Soho Theatre Bar. Contemporary, comfortable, air-conditioned and accessible, Soho Theatre is busy from early morning to late at night.

*'London's coolest theatre by a mile'* (Midweek)

21 Dean Street
London W1D 3NE
Admin: 020 7287 5060
Box Office: 0870 429 6883
www.sohotheatre.com

**Soho Theatre Bar**
Soho Theatre Bar is a comfortable and affordable place to meet in central London.

**The Terrace Bar**
The Terrace Bar on the second floor serves a range of soft and alcoholic drinks.

**Email information list**
For regular programme updates and offers visit www.sohotheatre.com

**Hiring the theatre**
Soho Theatre has a range of rooms and space for hire.  Please contact the theatre on 020 7287 5060 or go to www.sohotheatre.com for further details.

# ● soho theatre

## Staff

Artistic Director: Lisa Goldman
Executive Director: Mark Godfrey

### Board of Directors

Nicholas Allott – chair
Sue Robertson – vice chair
David Aukin
Norma Heyman
Roger Jospé
Jeremy King
Neil Mendoza
Simon Minty
Michael Naughton
David Pelham
Roger Wingate
Christopher Yu

### Honorary Patrons

Bob Hoskins – President
Peter Brook CBE
Simon Callow
Sir Richard Eyre CBE

### Artistic Team

Writers' Centre Director: Nina Steiger
Soho Connect Director: Suzanne Gorman
Casting Director: Nadine Hoare
International Associate: Paul Sirett
Artistic Associate: Esther Richardson
Director of Talks: Stephanie Merritt
Writers' Centre Assistant: Sheena
Bucktowonsing
Senior Reader: Dale Heinan

### Administration

General Manager: Catherine Thornborrow
Deputy General Manager: Erin Gavaghan
Assistant to Artistic Director
& Executive Director: Nicola Edwards
Financial Controller: Kevin Dunn
Book Keeper: Elva Tehan

### Marketing, Development and Press

Marketing and Development Directors:
Elizabeth Duducu, Jacqui Gellman
Development Manager: Zoe Crick
Marketing Manager: Nicki Marsh
Press and Public Relations: Nancy Poole
(020 7478 0142)
Development Assistant: Zebina Nelson-Myrie
Marketing and New Media Assistant:
Alex Fleming
Access Officer: Charlie Swinbourne

### Box Office and Front of House

Front of House Manager: Jennifer Dromey
Box Office and Audience
Development Manager: Steve Lock
Deputy Box Office Manager: Danielle Baker
Box Office Assistants: Lou Beere, Philip Elvy,
Tamsin Flessey, Lynne Forbes, Louise Green,
Eniola Jaiyeoba, Helen Matthews, Leah Read,
Becca Savory, Traci Leigh Scarlett, Nida Vohra,
Tom Webb and Natalie Worrall.
Duty Managers: Colin Goodwin, Martin
Murphy and Michael Owen.
Front of House staff: Carla Almeida, Beth
Aynsley, Paul Griffiths, Louise Hall, Juliette
Haygarth, Kyle Jenkins, Touy Dinh Le, Kate
Mulley, Camilla Read, Monique Sterling,
Gemma Strong, Stephanie Thomas and
Nida Vohra.

### Production

Production Manager: Matt Noddings
Technical Manager: Nick Blount
Head of Lighting: Christoph Wagner
Technician: Natalie Smith

## THE SOHO THEATRE DEVELOPMENT CAMPAIGN

Soho Theatre receives core funding from Arts Council England, London.

In order to provide as diverse a programme as possible and expand our audience development and outreach work, we rely upon additional support from trusts and foundations, individuals and businesses. All of our major sponsors share a common commitment to developing new areas of activity and encouraging creative partnerships between business and the arts. We are immensely grateful for the invaluable support from our sponsors and donors and wish to thank them for their continued commitment.

Soho Theatre has a Friends Scheme in support of its education programme and work developing new writers and reaching new audiences. To find out how to become a Friend of Soho Theatre, contact the development department on 020 7478 0109, email development@sohotheatre.com or visit www.sohotheatre.com.

**Sponsors:** Angels, The Costumiers, Bloomberg, TEQUILA\London, Rathbones.

**Principal Supporters and Education Patrons:** Anonymous · The City Bridge Trust · The Ernest Cook Trust · Tony and Rita Gallagher · Nigel Gee · The Paul Hamlyn Foundation · Roger Jospé · Jack and Linda Keenan · John Lyon's Charity · Man Group plc Charitable Trust · Sigrid Rausing · The Rose Foundation · Carolyn Ward · The Harold Hyam · Wingate Foundation

**Soho Business Members:** Goodman Derrick · The Groucho Club · Ronnie Scott's Jazz Club

**Trusts and Foundations:** Anonymous · The Carr-Gregory Trust · Miss Hazel Wood Charitable Trust · Hyde Park Place Estate Charity · The Kobler Trust · The Mackintosh Foundation · Teale Charitable Trust

**Dear Friends:** Anonymous · Jill and Michael Barrington · David Day · John Drummond · Madeleine Hamel · Jane and Andrew McManus · Michael and Mimi Naughton · Hannah Pierce · Nicola Stanhope · Alex Vogel

**Good Friends and Friends:** Thank you also to the many Soho Friends we are unable to list here. For a full list of our patrons, please visit www.sohotheatre.com.

Registered Charity: 267234

POLISH CULTURAL INSTITUTE

The aim of the **Polish Cultural Institute** is to bring contemporary Polish culture to British audiences. From art, film and theatre to music, literature and even videogames, the PCI's events are held at leading venues in London and across the UK.

Theatre is one of Poland's greatest exports, and the Dorota Masłowska play which you are experiencing tonight is a fine example.

Last year, Poland had an immense presence at Edinburgh Festival Fringe, with celebrated shows such as *Macbeth: Who is that Bloodied Man*, *Carmen Funebre* and *The Table* (which transfered to the Tricycle Theatre), to name but a few. The PCI firmly intends to make 2008 Poland's greatest year in Edinburgh yet.

For more information on all **PCI** events, please visit: **www.PolishCulture.org.uk**

# KINOTEKA

THE 6TH POLISH FILM FESTIVAL

While many exciting Polish productions will grace the London stage in 2008, the **Polish Cultural Institute** is equally proud to announce this year's **KINOTEKA 6th Polish Film Festival**.

**KINOTEKA** will be held at such prestigious venues as Riverside Studios, the Barbican, the Prince Charles Cinema and BFI Southbank…

The festival's larger-than-ever programme will launch with the UK premiere of acclaimed theatre and film actor/director Jerzy Stuhr's latest film, *Twists of Fate,* on 10 April at Riverside Studios. In addition to a dozen Polish films in the programme, **KINOTEKA** will feature Ken Loach's *It's a Free World*, which was partly shot in Poland, and a tribute to the late director Jerzy Kawalerowicz.

From the latest award-winning films and world premieres to Q&As with the stars and an exhibition of **Andrzej Klimowski**'s renowned film posters, **KINOTEKA** will give Londoners a unique look at the best in Polish cinema today. For more information on **KINOTEKA** and a detailed programme please visit:
**www.kinoteka.org.uk**

A COUPLE OF POOR, POLISH-SPEAKING ROMANIANS

First published as *Dwoje biednych Rumunów mówiących po polsku*
by Lampa i Iskra Boża in 2006.

This translation published in 2008 by Oberon Books Ltd
521 Caledonian Road, London N7 9RH
Tel: 020 7607 3637 / Fax: 020 7607 3629
e-mail: info@oberonbooks.com
www.oberonbooks.com

A catalogue record for this book is available from the British
Library.

ISBN: 978-1-84002-846-1

Cover illustration by Andrzej Klimowski

Printed in Great Britain by Antony Rowe Ltd, Chippenham

# Characters

PARCHA

DŻINA

DRIVER

POLICEMAN

BARTENDER

HALINA

WIESIEK

WOMAN DRIVER

OLD MAN

WAITER

MAN 1

MAN 2

MAN 3

WOMAN 1

WOMAN 2

CREW / PASSENGERS

# Prologue

*Voices from nowhere.*

PARCHA: Martini rose, martini bianco, martini cough.
Martini rose, seicento, los trabantos, buenos aires.
Fiat uno, cinquecento, seicento, fellatio.
Mirel matie, cantare, romy schneider, coffee and tea.

MAN 1: (*Gangster.*) He's belting out this bollocks; she says
'Shut Up!' 'But darlin'' he goes, 'this is our Romanian
national anthem, do not renounce tradition!' You can still
see the scratches – they grabbed hold of it really hard,
and when I took off, they scraped the paint. Metallic
black!

DRIVER: This weird thing happened, when I was driving
from Warsaw to Elbląg*, these oddly behaved people
introduced themselves... 'We're from Romania, I can
show you a flag.' But what flag? What flag?

MAN 1: I said, 'What scraps of meat? What fucking scraps
of meat? Tell you what, put your little friend in my car,
give me your address and I'll send you back the scraps of
meat. You can have yourself a sandwich. NOW GET THE
FUCK OUT!'

MAN 2: Me and the wife stopped at the garage, the Orlen,
and this very bizarre couple approached us, one of them,
a woman, she's pregnant...and shouting that they're
Polish-speaking Romanians. My wife's undergoing
chemotherapy, one tit gone already, I never remember if
it's the left or the right, and...

MAN 1: But just like a girl, she grabs hold and won't let go,
not even when I move the car. And I go, 'No! No fucking
way.'

WOMAN 1: It's disgusting. It's appalling.

MAN 2: I couldn't let them in, officer. As a law-abiding citizen
I told them, I just can't.

* Pronounced 'El-blong'

WOMAN 1: And she looked away so strangely. Really. Like a fish in aspic. My husband said that unfortunately it wasn't possible to let them in, but they were really pushy. When we refused, they started crying and pleading.

DRIVER: I just said no. No. Because no, no.

MAN 1: So the silly bitch fell on her arse, it was her own fault. She fell on her arse, and I said, come on slut, come play in the traffic, I'll iron you flat! And I'm driving straight towards her, and man, she was running –

MAN 3: Having stopped to refuel, I went in to pay and upon returning, my son – who is ten years old, proceeded to ask if there was such a thing as Polish-speaking Romanians. I told him of course not, but he's a bit slow for his age, you see, and he makes stuff up.

WOMAN 2: They seemed so nice, so nice, but when we saw the terrible state of their teeth, then no, I flatly refused to give them a lift. I'm not saying it's a big thing, but it's not really such a challenge to buy a cheap toothbrush and brush your teeth twice a day, (*Singing.*) wishy-washy, up-down, swill it round and that's that. You have to take care of them. It's such a pleasure. Ahhmenn.

# Act One

## SCENE 1

*Winter, petrol station, getting dark, two poor Romanians are trying to get themselves into the DRIVER's car.*

PARCHA: Wife is called Dżina.

DRIVER: So this girl, about twenty, pregnant, she didn't say a word, she just sat there, but I worked out she's an accomplice to the murder. Whose murder? Me, my murder, mine! Strange though it may seem.

PARCHA: Just call her Dżina. Dżina, what's your last name?

DRIVER: When asked for a surname, she continued to make no response, no comment, but her name Dżina is probably short for Regina, (*Sings the funeral service.*) and in fact this is the clue which could easily lead you to both murderers, because it's a rare name, Dżina. So I demand that you capture these assassins in the name of all taxpayers who might also be attacked and killed by them.

PARCHA: She doesn't have a last name. Simply Dżina. It's a beautiful name for such a girl, actually, to have only one name, like some kind of pop star. Dżina is a good Girl-ina. No stealing, no barfing, I swear by this innocent child that she carries in her belly. You know, this is life! We are poor, honest, Polish-speaking Romanians. My wife is pregnant, she is going to Wrocław to visit a doctor, a specialist, because she has these metastases, cysts, it's just a mess there in her belly. Etcetera... So we'll all go together, then – to wherever you're going?

DRIVER: To Wrocław! You get that, officer, and this is on the road to Gdańsk!

PARCHA: To Wrocław, but we're not insisting. It might even be better in Gdańsk, there are many specialists, the sea, iodine, shells, ships. Gdańsk is okay, I don't want to fight about it.

DRIVER: I told them I'm going nowhere. Only to Elbląg, and back, I told them calmly, told them the truth, because that's the way I am, calm.

PARCHA: So let's go to Elbow or wherever, she'll deal with it, deal with it she always does. We Romanians, woa! We're a feisty people. She'll sing you something, when she sobers up, right Dżina? You know the way, sugar. A very nice girl. Go on, sit down this way, right? This way, my beautiful gorgeous. Everything all right? D'you have a new scrunchie? But when did you buy it? Just now? I can't believe it. She's gorgeous, you know? Are these rhubarbs, these stones?

DRIVER: Hard to say how it happened – it only took a moment. The man she was with, I knew his face from somewhere, one of these famous gangsters, I'm sure. Beefburger or the other one. So I turned around, when I heard him shout: 'Watch out! The scrounging Romanian Bastards are coming!' Or something like that. But of course, it was a set-up and he bundled her into my passenger seat, with all these bags and I say: Whhhaaat? And he goes: Dżina. This is Dżina. I felt concern, officer, which in my opinion is understandable. I say: What Dżina, what about Dżina, what do I care about someone's wife called Dżina? She could be Princess fucking Diana, I don't give a shit. Just get her out, I'm late for work. What the fuck-gut is going on?!

PARCHA: To be honest, her real name is Pyralgina, but she tells everyone to call her Dżina. Pyralgina, Codeinea, Aspirina, Caffeina…these are traditional Romanian female names. In Romania, Saint Peralgina was the patron saint of drunk girls coming home in the dark. Right? Shit happens. Girls like her. But she tells everyone that she is Dżina, some sort of caprice on her part. Don't call her Pyrangina, show respect for feelings, call her Dżina, please, this perhaps great artist.

DRIVER: Who gives a shit?! Out, filthy Romanians, or I'll call…

Meantime, his pregnant sidekick, the one I described earlier, pretended not to hear and there was this Christmas tree car freshener dangling, and she was playing with it, probably planning how to nick it without me noticing.

And he tells me to look at her and see how pretty she is, and what do I care, pretty or not? All I know is that she smells stale like fried oil. Piss off with your Princess Margerina and her tub of scraps! I'm not going anywhere.

DŻINA: You said you're going.

DRIVER: Yes, I made a mistake. I said this ironically. Because I was a getting a little freaked-out by this hostile situation.

DŻINA: This thing is fucking wild.

DRIVER: And the girl, this bimbo, still taking the piss, toying with the Christmas tree.

DŻINA: Did you buy it or did you make it yourself?

DRIVER: How made it?! How: made it myself?! Did I cut it out of a carpet? You can buy them anywhere, go in the garage there, it's full of them! What fucking planet did you drop down from?

PARCHA: Look at her, how pretty she is. My little rapscallion. Well, her teeth are a joke, but it was hard life that did it, isn't it, darling? Romania knows no mercy. All our lives, we've been eating scraps of meat, it destroys the bones. And rubies, I mean rhubarb and for sweets we liked Rennies. (*Burps.*)

DRIVER: And he's off on his spaced-out odyssey, how they ate burrs, weeds and rocks back in this Romania place. Well maybe they did, but hey we had martial law, we had food stamps. JESUS! Stop talking to me! I'm not listening to you! I've done listening. Not listening.

*He covers his ears in a dramatic gesture.*

DŻINA: Or icing sugar. Or vitamin powder, Visolvit, you remember, a rare, rare treat and only when Mum pawned the family crystal, we had a stack of that, because she whittled vegetables all round Romania and was very famous.

PARCHA: I'm not hiding anything, that's the pot calling the kettle black, you know this famous Romanian saying? I've got big bad teeth with gaps for the sunny spells.

DRIVER: And he's showing me his teeth, these crooked brown pegs, looking like cigarette stubs and I almost puked, how can you have such teeth and still procreate...? And that bloated bitch with the Christmas tree? Is that any way to behave?

DŻINA: Wow, I'd love to have such a thing...

DRIVER: Then he says.

PARCHA: So take it, he's got two, he won't mind, right?

DRIVER: You hear that? He told her to go ahead and take it. My property, my little tree. Strangers I never met before in my life.

DŻINA: (*Trying to hang the Christmas tree on her neck.*) But where should I hang it?

PARCHA: You know: she can be stubborn. She's stubborn because she's stubborn. Give it to her, do it FOR ME. We don't have these trees in Romania; we don't have such trees as Christmas trees, only these other ones. Oak. Croak.

DRIVER: Croak! Have you ever heard of a Croak tree, officer? Because I haven't! Please leave the premises of my car. Just leave me alone. Take old fatty guts and fuck off, this is my car, I got no time for this. So I tried to drag her out of the car: Get out, bitch!!! She acts like she's just woken up:

DŻINA: How could you?!!

DRIVER: And she grabs her bag and here, she punches me here, in the neck.

DŻINA: You bully, mind those pig-trotters.

DRIVER: Not far from the place where I have a cancerous boil, that could have caused an irreversible threat to my health, to my life. I started screaming: People! People! Help! I'm trying to call for help, but they won't let me, terrorising me and then trying to kill me.

PARCHA: Man, have you lost it or what? Beating up a pregnant woman, a big guy like you? Can't you see she's shorter, thinner, she doesn't stand a chance? Stay where you are, Jean Genie, don't you worry, unzip your boots, that's right, my little sundial, you've got a bogey in your nose, you know? Dżina is walking around with boogie-woogies in her nose. So sweet. Here, let me get that for you.

DŻINA: No-o! Myself!

PARCHA: No, let me do it. LET ME DO IT. Here we go!

DRIVER: And he actually shows me her snot, this disgusting snot from her nose. Now I'm very sensitive to this sort of thing, it takes me right back to primary school, the boys with their spit and their yellow ear wax and setting their farts on fire... NO I'M NOT GOING! NOT GOING ANYWHERE! I'M SITTING! Sitting in my car! Sitting! Taking in the view! Because I like winter!

PARCHA: It's your choice, I've asked nicely, and now I'm going to kill you.

*PARCHA pulls out a penknife.*

DRIVER: It was then that he threatened to take my life.

PARCHA: I'm killing you, though I don't really want to and to be honest I don't know how. I don't know the proper technique, so it'll probably be more painful than any pain you've yet to experience. And then you'll go to hell, good luck! You're stuck in hell, balls on fire, really not cool. And you'll think to yourself, was it worth it? Really it wasn't worth it, after all I was only going to Oblong, and now I'm stuffed. Don't put an innocent man behind bars – meaning me.

DŻINA: And this guy thought he was the man, like he'd been on a 'no-more Mr Nice Guy' course. But flash a potato peeler in his face and he poos his pants.

PARCHA: You've no idea where this knife has been. Maybe I
scraped the fish tank with it. Or maybe I cut dog shit into
slices, eh? Or maybe it's completely blunt. Because it may
be my envelope-knife. Envelopes with letters in them.
From my family in Romania, letters written on tree bark,
with urine and faeces. And Easter-egg dye. I have little
cousins begging to be sent some sweetie bar wrappers in
those letters, Laszlo wants one from Snickers, and Ruchla
wants one from Mars, and Rakoczy wants Twix, and
Cincinnati dreams about one of those cardboard shovels
for Freedom Fries, you know the ones I mean? And d'you
think I send them this stuff; do I send it? I do. It really
matters to them, really a lot.

*Holding the knife, he opens the back door and gets into the car.*

Get in, I tell you. Get in and no bullshit. Get in get in get
in. We Romanians are very patient, but in the end any
Romanian will tell you: Enough. Let's go.

## SCENE 2

*They are driving.*

*DŻINA and PARCHA are taking out cigarettes and are smoking at
a great pace, two cheap cigarettes at a time; choking.*

PARCHA: Enough! Lucky I didn't kill you in the end, though
I was on the edge, I'd have been so depressed in the
morning, know what I mean? It was a really nice party,
and then I go and kill some guy, some stranger I never
met before! Ugggh – horrible feeling. Faster, friend,
faster. Let's respect each other's time. But chill out will
you. If you sweat so much the cold wind will get you here.

*He massages the DRIVER's back with feeling.*

Seicento. Nice wheels. Right, Dżina?

DŻINA: It's fast as a bullet, isn't it? Nothing can stop this car.

PARCHA: Or the Daewoo Tico. Now that's a car. Man, when
we tell them in Romania what we've been driving then,
whoaaaaaa! Our relatives will burn down our hut out of
jealousy. Seicento. It's not a car, it's a religion. People

go farting along in these other cars.... There! See what I mean! This one, fuck! Fuck me! Overtake him! You're driving like some pussy, like a right cunt... You got a car with such potential and you're moving in slow motion, like those naked bitches mud wrestling. Dżinny is going to puke...

DŻINA: Oy you, I don't think I'm that drunk. (*She burps.*)

DRIVER: (*Getting increasingly hysterical.*) My assailants were constantly humiliating me, rushing me, forcing me to drive faster and faster against the highway code. I've been driving for 19 years and I have this compulsion: when I see a car coming towards me, I read its license plate, I just can't stop myself. The same with the road signs, Gdańsk 153km, etc, Iława, etc. I add all them all up and divide them by the number of signs. I pray it comes out even. When it's even, then I'm happy. For me, it's proof of the existence of some sort of symmetry and order at the most fundamental level of cosmic chaos. So if it's an odd number, it's very bad.

PARCHA: I'm taking off my shoes, okey-doke? Perke? Puertoricos? Martini seicento fellatio?

DRIVER: I'm staying silent. Not rising to the bait. Whatever you do, don't let the killer provoke up.

PARCHA: What I've just said means 'big up, bro' in Romanian. But I've had these kiddie-slippers on for too long. Oh-oh...! It may be a little suffo-porno-cating... But we're among friends right?

*He is yawning, getting ready to go to sleep.*

DRIVER: I just kept repeating to myself: it's nothing, it's nothing. It's nothing nothing, nothing. Perhaps it isn't even happening. Perhaps it's just a dream and I'm getting all nervous quite unnecessarily. But it wasn't a dream. And now he's falling asleep, a little less asleep and I had hoped... I wondered...

PARCHA: Ugh, what a vile stench, Dżina, did you fart?

DŻINA: I didn't fart, the smell was already here when we got in.

PARCHA: Right. It stinks really bad. But it wasn't me.

DŻINA: Yeah. Me neither.

PARCHA: Someone's got a marshy arse, that's for sure. But it wasn't me.

DŻINA: It surely wasn't me. It wasn't you and it wasn't me so I don't know who. But someone let rip.

PARCHA: You pervy piggy. Silent but violent. Well well well…

DRIVER: (*Getting hysterical.*) Whhaattt? IT WASN'T ME!

DŻINA: Then who did?

PARCHA: YOU! It was you. No one else!

DŻINA: Stinker!

*The* DRIVER *is hysterically trying to grab a phone and make a phone call.*

PARCHA: And what are you planning to do with that? Go on, who you gonna call? The police? Call yourself a friend? Give me back the phone. Give it me.

*Pause.*

You're driving; this is outrageously dangerous. So I'll dial it for you, and you can just say: Hurry please! It's an emergency. I've got this pregnant woman in the car! She's freezing and helpless! And so I'm giving her a lift somewhere! Help! I don't know what I'm doing! Help!

You people. You unused fucks. How can you?

*He lies down with the mobile and falls asleep.*

DRIVER: And finally, he fell asleep. And I took my chance with the woman. Being a woman made her more human. Women can't be evil – unlike men. That's how the world keeps going I think, because they have to give birth to children, and they're not alcoholics, so I held out some hope, and I asked her – cat got your tongue?

DŻINA: I learned to talk, you know? But it didn't work out. I never had the knack.

PARCHA: (*Dreaming.*) We are only poor, honest Polish-speaking Romanians... We came here by The Ibuprofen. We don't have such Christmas trees. Only different trees.

DRIVER: Is this your boyfriend then?

DŻINA: Who? Him? No, he's my cousin. So we're sort of lovers.

DRIVER: He snores a bit, this Romanian of yours, doesn't he?

PARCHA: (*Dreaming.*) It's because of the snout.

DŻINA: It's because of the snout. He had his nose broken in prison. He's got a massive complex about it. Don't mention it again or he'll chop us into dogmeat for conspiring against him.

PARCHA: (*Dreaming.*) No, no, no, no... Hold it, what's going on?

*Pause.*

DRIVER: (*Wiping his face with a handkerchief.*) Is it his baby?

DŻINA: Whose?

DRIVER: Your kid?

DŻINA: My kid with him?

DRIVER: Well, you know, are you pregnant because of him?

DŻINA: Meeee? Aaaaah, this! Noooooo, no, of course not!

DRIVER: Not his then?

DŻINA: No, I met him yesterday... Anyway it doesn't matter. You sound like my mum, I tell her: this is a child, just a child and that's it, d'you get me? This is my son. Shit happens, but you're not the father. And she goes: well you should take care of it then. But oh no. You smoke, drink, booze, open your legs for anyone passing. Surface at five in the afternoon and surprise-surprise, you're none too lively. Do something useful for a change, tidy up... And I...

Okay, it doesn't matter. Right. Thanks for reminding me.

*She takes out a can of glue; pretends to sniff it.*

I'm completely addicted to this shit. Truth is I don't even like it.

DRIVER: And this monster, this terrible woman, I'm not even going to call her a woman. She takes a can of glue! And she's looking at herself in the lid! Like a mirror!

PARCHA: (*Dreaming.*) Dżina is an artist.

DRIVER: And this, t-t-that, isn't it bad for the child?

DŻINA: No way... I got it under control now. Anyhow, the doctors say because my child is used to it, if I come off it now, it'll be a worse shock than the odd little binge. And he could be retarded, he could go crazy in there, so it's better for him that I sniff a bit than be in a bad mood. It's supposed to be quite healthy when absorbed in small quantities. Have a little sniff, you could relax a bit and not be so. Oooh, here come the lovely tanks, there's going to be war.

DRIVER: Noooo! Never!

I screamed. The stench was terrible, I started to feel dizzy.

DŻINA: You know what? The worst fucking thing is that the world wants to turn you into a grey rag, saluting in a line, a passerby passing across the street. The passenger of a fucking tram, swaying like a limp flag, a face without features, without a face. Just like you. Cold-cuts man. I don't want to be like that. (*Terrified.*) Hey, what's-yer-name, turn around! Turn around! And tell me something.

DRIVER: What d'you mean? What's happening?

DŻINA: Tell me something, but do it so that she doesn't see, you understand? No! Not like that, don't stare! That's my mother, right? Sitting in the back? Just tell me, because I can't look. Brunette, fifties.

DRIVER: Nooooo. That's your boyfriend, the one you started with! Your cousin!

DŻINA: That bitch is following me. I just blew a month's child maintenance and she's really gonna kill me now. I can't turn around because she'll pop up screaming: 'Do something useful like tidy up, this is your son.'

DRIVER: But who? Him?! (*Pointing at PARCHA.*)

DŻINA: My son? You've completely lost it haven't you! Fuck I don't feel well. Maybe I'm in labour. Call Dr Who!

DRIVER: (*Almost crying.*) How? Your cousin took my phone!

DŻINA: Chill out will you. If that's the case, I'll just hold it in. Ha Ha... Fuck me, you were really freaking out...

*They are driving.*

DRIVER: It's not a joke, you know. When my wife was in labour, there were complications, her anus was torn apart, her bladder damaged, women can really have a bad...

PARCHA: (*Already awake.*) Dżina doesn't have an anus.

DRIVER: Of course she doesn't... I wasn't suggesting...

PARCHA: Dżina doesn't have an anus, she's not that kind of girl.

DŻINA: Shut the fuck up, will you? Go back to sleep, you're interrupting a civilised conversation.

PARCHA: Shut yourself up, you. Don't tell me what to do when he insults you...

DŻINA: Dick. Fuck. Shit.

PARCHA: Turd. Shit. Super shit-storm. Pussy. Armpit.

DRIVER: (*On the verge of a breakdown.*) Stop it...FOR GOD'S SAKE... People...! Do you have to be so offensive? Call each other names?! And make such a racket! Woman, you're pregnant, but you sniff glue, curse, fill the car with the stench, your poor baby hearing and seeing everything. In foetal life, he can memorise things! It'll come out one day in front of your guests! The first word he's going to say will be... God...

PARCHA: Hear that, you old slapper? Please excuse her, she's only a stupid Romanian. Spent her whole life in the monkey and dog factory and she doesn't know how to behave among people. See what you've done? The man almost had a heart attack, listening to your bullshit.

DŻINA: Yours ain't any better!

PARCHA: No, I was just say…

DŻINA: No. No. No and once again, no.

PARCHA: Yes. Yes, exactly!

DRIVER: (*Bursts out crying and stops the car.*) Stop! I beg you… You have it… I can't go on. Not going! I'm giving you this… This car is yours… I'm giving it to you! I'm getting out… I'll walk… I feel like walking, here in this forest, that's the place for me. I'll find some old root and I'll build a house in it… I'll carve out the plates myself, the spoons, the hooks, these…these musical instruments…

PARCHA: No no no, my dear, it's out of the question. Stop wailing and calm down. Calm down at once. We all have deadlines, we're in a hurry too.

DŻINA: No, let him cry, let him cry. Let him have a good cry.

PARCHA: Don't defend him.

DŻINA: Cry man, cry, it's purifying. I remember having cystitis, you know how it is. I just couldn't sit still, I wanted to pee all the time. I'm flying, running! Peeing my pants! Going for gold for Romanian women with a bladder infection! I'm trying to undo my fly! I am all covered in pee! I sit on the throne and triumphantly squeeze out three hot drops and I feel as if someone was knitting me together right then and there – at the end of knitting needles. You know. Sewing my dead body together on a sewing machine. Something like an orgasm. But more painful.

DRIVER: (*Cries all the time.*) Officer, the fact that I'm alive I owe solely to my ability to stay cool under stress, I didn't let them get to me, all this time I didn't react to their attempts to deprive me of my sanity, because now I have no doubt… And then I saw a police car ahead. For a moment I thought it was a mirage, that they'd planted it there while plotting my downfall, to provoke me, to incite me, and then just to laugh at me, sneer at me...

PARCHA: Oh what the, fuck, the pigs, you see what you've done now? Noooo, come on man, this is not friendship, what you're doing now is right out of fucking order.

DRIVER: And then, I don't even know, it took seconds. Despite the assassins' threats and accusations and trying to guilt trip me over the patrol car to make me drive on, I managed to veer over, in the direction of the police...

POLICEMAN: What are you doing? Why are you stopping?

DRIVER: I was going too fast, Sergeant, Sergeant Major, arrest me, I, me – there, where you can't see, there, over that hill, I was overtaking while driving up that hill, on a double, continuous line, I hit somebody, you didn't see it, but I admit to everything – and more, please arrest me now, I'm willing to accept the punishment. Please arrest me, it's all I ask, I'll fill you in on the details later...

PARCHA: Ddddad... Dad, please come back to the car.

POLICEMAN: Whhaaat? What's this all about? What's going on?

PARCHA: Everything is absolutely fine. We are poor, honest, Polish-speaking Romanians, my dad has Alzheimer's, there's a plague of it in Romania. It's pretty scary driving with him. Since he left the camp, he's not himself at all. Always having nightmares about the trenches.

DRIVER: I didn't make a note of the number plate of the two policemen, but you'd find them easily enough. One's not too tall, the other's blond, a bit taller. I think they should be suspended for failing to help a hostage or even for conspiring with thieves and killers, and believing their nasty lies about me being in the trenches and losing my identity there.

POLICEMAN: (*To PARCHA.*) The concern is whether he's safe to drive.

PARCHA: Sergeant, as regards that. Are we on the right road to Elbląg, I mean, are we heading in the right direction?

Because Dad is confused and me and my sister, we don't know the way at all and we're in a hurry to catch a boat to Romania. I mean the coal barge called The Ibuprofen. Have you heard of it?

POLICEMAN:But there's no sea at Elbląg.

PARCHA: That's right. Because it sails on a lake. The Elbląskie lake.

DRIVER: A coal barge called The Ibuprofen. That's the terrible name they mentioned. Please track it down. They might still be on it.

## SCENE 3

*They drive on. The* DRIVER *is driving, sobbing hysterically over the steering wheel.*

PARCHA: STOP BAWLING!

DŻINA: Leave him alone...

PARCHA: I'll start crying if he doesn't stop.

DŻINA: Let him cry, get it out of his system.

PARCHA: No. Dżinny, I can't work under these hysterical conditions.

DRIVER: The poor winter sun dropped behind the horizon like a crappy little coin. The road was full of the rolling corpses of runover dogs and other animals, wild and domestic. There were last year's ice cream ads swaying in the wind outside old bars, faded by the greedy looks of children. I saw darkness. I touched it.

PARCHA: MA-AN. Listen to me. Look we're really grateful to you for giving us a lift. It's been a long time since we experienced such kindness from a stranger, who didn't have to be so nice to us, who didn't have to help us out. But he wanted to do it and he did. This humanity, this generosity of spirit, it means a lot to us...

*He starts rummaging through her bags.*

So we'll be on our way. The coal barge isn't far. Your offer of a lift and the fact that you did it of your own free will, was a great help to us. Thanks to you we will soon be in our homeland. A Romanian doesn't bullshit, this is our motto. So we would like to reward your goodness and kindness.

*The DRIVER looks at PARCHA with disbelief; PARCHA takes a roll of banknotes and other things out of a plastic bag.*

I'm the wizard of the most beautiful fairy tale in the world. I came to Warsaw dressed in disguise to see if people are good and do good deeds. Look there's five grand here, this is your reward. One, two, four, five. And my MP3 player. And three Euros. And my shades... Oh maybe not my shades, I'll be needing them tomorrow.

You know how it works. There's a switch here by the headphones. You download different music off the internet. You move it from the computer and you can have five thousand MP3s on there. I've already stored some albums on it, but I'm not sure if you'll like them. I wish I'd thought about this earlier. If I'd known, I would've downloaded some stuff especially for you, you know, Wojciech Gąssowski, Koń Polski, De Mono, Kabaret Otto, Neil Diamond, that sort of thing.

So, we'll be going. Come on, Dżina, get your shit together. This is real money, not some fake that's been copied on a copy machine. You buy something nice with it. Buy a Thermomix... We recommend it. Dżina and I have one in Romania and it's really worth having. It bakes bread by itself. Dżina goes to the field in the morning, gathers the grain. Then we mix it in the Thermomix and we get this bread, this fantastically fresh bread, without any of those E1939s and E1968's. It's such a PLEASURE.

DŻINA: Hey, are you crazy? I'm shagged as a rug, and there's only forest and blackcurrants out there.

PARCHA: LET'S GO.

*They go.*

DRIVER: And, Officer, they saved the worst till last. He held his knife at my throat and demanded money and car keys. And she was pointing at me with a handgun that she took from her bag – cocked no doubt. They were out to kill and rob me. They demanded valuables, jewellery, electronic equipment and kitchen appliances, to be specific they demanded a Thermomix, which I don't even own and never have. My mother-in-law had one, but we're not on speaking terms, how did they even know about it. How? I think they must have followed me. For many years I've suspected I was being watched. Then they ran into the forest without a word, without so much as a thank you. They didn't even leave me any money, not a grosz, not one zloty. And, Officer, I want this added to the files, that if they are caught, I hope I'll be allowed to look them in the eye. But I won't forgive them. I won't. I won't. No, never. Did you write that down? I won't. Good.

*End of Act One.*

# Act Two

## SCENE 1

*Evening. DŻINA and PARCHA are walking along the road, crying, in a complete psycho-physical mess.*

PARCHA: Please. Please. Please. Stop rubbing up against me when you walk, I'm sensitive to that kind of thing. But why? Why?

Five thousand and an MP3 player?! How come? Gave him? Gave who? That lunatic? You're joking! Me? I gave it to him? For free? But he was seriously deranged, that man! So you didn't say anything to stop me? Why did I say I was the wizard of the most beautiful fairy tale? What wizard? Maybe you told him that? But me?

OK, I do remember this feeling of being a wizard, but I can't believe you just stood by, watched me give him five grand and did absolutely nothing. When you're cleaned out, as well. Have you completely lost it, woman? You think I found it under the Christmas tree? I worked my arse off for that money. And I gave it to him? Maybe I sold it? Maybe I sold him the money? No, that makes no sense. No sense at all.

Where's that bag? Sorry. Dżina. What sort of a name is that anyway? Couldn't they have come up with anything better? Are you Native American? Peruvian? And your surname is Magdelina? Dżina Bagdelina? I'm sorry, ha! You have to give me that, in the deepest shit of my life, at the chasm's edge, at the lowest fucking point, my sense of humour still radiates.

No, no, no, let's calm down, establish the facts. No need to get all emotional about it. So there was a party, that's a fact. We got a bit pissed – I think that must have been when I met you. But those fucking drugs man... 'Just say no!' I can't remember a thing. You could sell me any story. Like where the hell did I get five grand? From the bank? Okay.

Impossible. No way. I would've remembered. I gave it to him? All of it? And you let me do it? And not even ten zlotys left?! Look there, in the bag, there must be something. I need a coffee, got to freshen up, take a shower. Give me a mirror, I have to be at work at eight tomorrow. And what about my MP3 player? I can't believe I gave him that as well? I had everything on there, all my favourite songs. And where's my mobile? Haven't you got it? Check the bag, it must be there. And my driver's licence! How come they're not there? What do you mean not there? Give it to me. They must be there.

So you jacked them, eh? Don't be offended, I'm only asking, I don't know you from Adam. I don't trust anybody any more. I have to be at work at eight tomorrow. On set at eight tomorrow, do you understand? Do you understand what that means? On set at eight and when I don't fucking show up, all that's left will be the tears. Do you work anywhere? Do you even know what that means?

DŻINA: No.

PARCHA: So where did you get the money for this wonderful party then? Was it my generosity again?

DŻINA: I don't know, I got it out the cashpoint.

PARCHA: Oh, it flew in there all the way from heaven, just for you…?

DŻINA: Nooo, it was probably the child maintenance.

PARCHA: What child maintenance?

DŻINA: Well, when I went to the cashpoint, I thought that there was nothing in there, but there it was, five hundred. So I think it was the child maintenance. So I bought myself a kebab and a few other things, and then there was this party…

PARCHA: Whoa whoa whoa, what child maintenance? Child maintenance for a child?

DŻINA: Yes, child maintenance for a child.

PARCHA: So where's the child?

DŻINA: What child?

PARCHA: Well I don't know, this child of yours, as far as I remember, you said you had a child.

DŻINA: Yes, that's right...

PARCHA: That's right. That's right. You have a child.

DŻINA: I left him somewhere. Wait. I must have walked him to nursery, right?

PARCHA: But when?

DŻINA: Well, I don't know. In the morning.

PARCHA: What do you mean in the morning? What morning?!

DŻINA: Yeah, that's right...

PARCHA: When exactly?

DŻINA: The day before yesterday, I s'pose. No, I mean yesterday, I s'pose. It was yesterday, yeah? Because it seems a bit unlikely that it was today.

PARCHA: And what then? Is he still there? Ha, ha.

DŻINA: Listen, you got anything to drink?

PARCHA: Now don't go beating yourself up about it, I'm only asking. Look, I don't give a shit about it, I don't even know you.

DŻINA: Well how am I supposed to know what happened? Maybe my mum picked him up. She does that sometimes when I can't.

PARCHA: That's great.

DŻINA: Don't ask me about things I can't change now.

PARCHA: You're right.

DŻINA: It's important he doesn't get bored. It's good for him to play Heroes by himself, spend some time on his own.

PARCHA: (*Starts screaming.*) That's right! That's right! On his own! And five thousand gone to fuck and that's a fact. And that's the fucking end of it. An end to the parties, an end to the drugs, an end to the kind of wild fucking parties which end with me delirious and giving away five grand to some fucking old man with neurasthenia. And I wake up dressed in a cardigan, ripped off the back of some corpse in 1972 and it's just fucking great. For the last eight hours I've been pretending to be a Polish-speaking Romanian and describing the harmful effects of eating scraps of meat, but suddenly it turns out that I'm a drugged-up Pole on a comedown, a Polish-speaking Pole on a comedown and I wake up in some kind of field, in some fucking blackcurrant patch in East Bumblefuck on the border with Kazakhstan, in a Kazakhstani cardigan that stinks of moth balls and my teeth blacked out with marker pen that I can't wash off. And I have to be on set at fucking eight because the truth is I play this priest Father Grzegorz in *Plebania*, the much-loved Polish television series.

Father Grzegorz. On top form, as always.

*Pause.*

Those drugs are bad news. We... I just need to ask this one thing, it's very important to me. I mean, it's probably stupid, so please forgive me. Did I, did we, I mean, you and me, did we have sex? I'm only asking.

## SCENE 2

*The Welcome Grill. The female* BARTENDER *and* HALINA, *the cloakroom attendant, are watching TV. From outside we hear the approaching turmoil and commotion. Enter* PARCHA *and* DŻINA, *sweating, on the edge of madness.*

BARTENDER: So we're sitting there watching TV, minding our own, when I hear these screams outside, a right palaver. So I goes: What's going on, whose screaming out there? I bet it's those Bulgarian whores shooting worms out of their cunts again. So I'm off to check when, suddenly, the door bursts open, and this two-person isolation ward walks in, I don't know, drunk or fucked up on something, or maybe they had just escaped from the funny farm, they had all these plastic bags. And what we got here? A duchess with a double-barrel belly.

Can I help you?

DŻINA: I need lots of boiling water. I'm having a baby. You, Granny, tear up some sheets.

BARTENDER: And she points to Halina. Granny! And she's swinging her handbag. I say: We don't have boiling water. There's coffee, tea, we got borsht, French fries. Croquette. Like it says on the board.

DŻINA: I'll have the croquette.

PARCHA: No no, she's joking! We don't want anything. One moment ladies, please.

Look there. Hold this. Turn around and look there. Hold this, and don't say a word, I'll do the talking. You stay here, look there and don't move.

Ladies, I apologize on behalf of this unstable individual. She's not herself today. She's not even pregnant, you know, she's just stuffed a pillow up there, oh, ha ha.

And you can stop laughing, numbskull, because it hasn't really been funny for quite a while now. You're a psychojunkie. Still fucked in the head.

Pardon my French, ladies I'm terribly sorry but something's happened and I'm a little distressed. Might I kindly ask you: what charming town is this? Where are we?

BARTENDER: What town is this, and where are they! That's what he asks me! Ostróda.

HALINA: This is Ostróda.

PARCHA: Ohhh yes, Ostróda, of course, a beautiful town. So...is that more to the South, the North, or the East? It's completely slipped my mind.

BARTENDER: Well that depends.

PARCHA: I see. Yes of course. That's right. It depends.

Because you see, ladies, we're here by accident. It's not our fault, we're from Warsaw, we took a wrong turn, ended up here...

BARTENDER: Yeah, right. I'm from Warsaw too. Halina and all. We're all from Warsaw. We came here for the winter season. We just got back from a sleigh ride.

PARCHA: There you are. A sledge is a great thing. What wonderful sledging weather, with the horse snorting loudly. In the words of the poet. You know, the great poet.

But back to business, dear ladies, because, joking aside, I find myself here in uncertain circumstances and I must be at work for eight am tomorrow and I don't have my phone on me. And I need to make an important call.

I don't look like this, you know. I really don't. It's a disguise, a joke, a fancy dress party... And you know what, ladies, it all ended in tears. In real life I'm a professional actor. I play Father Grzegorz in the TV series, you must have seen me. Father Grzegorz, right? On top form, as always. Well it's me. D'you know what the time is?

BARTENDER: And we're in disguise as well, sir. Halina is really Crystal Carrington and I'm Barbara Cartland. The time is ten pm. As you can see on the clock there.

PARCHA: Ten pm. No way. I need to get my beauty sleep. I have to make a phone call. What a fucking nightmare. Dżina, for christssake do something. Tell them. Please tell them who I am. Go on. Spit it out.

DŻINA: I'll have the borscht, two portions.

PARCHA: Noooooo.

HALINA: Mr Wiesiuuuu!!!

PARCHA: Nooo, don't do that. What do I need Wiesiek for? Who the hell is Wiesiek? You just don't get my situation at all do you? Who is Wiesiek, what does Wiesiek mean to me? Peeeeople! People. For God's sake. I'm Father

Grzegorz. Help your fellow man, I have to be at fucking work by eight am tomorrow.

BARTENDER: At eight am, begging for scraps?

DŻINA: We Romanians are a feisty people.

PARCHA: And you can shut up... Please – just be quiet. Turn around. Turn around. Turn around there. You left your kid waiting at nursery. Stand there and contemplate if that was motherly behaviour. She left her child in nursery. Three days ago. Spent the child maintenance on drugs. And a kebab. A psychopath, and a drug addict.

BARTENDER: And what's she talking about? That you're some kind of Romanians? It just gets better and better, doesn't it?

DŻINA: But my mum would have picked him up, I'm sure.

BARTENDER: The cheapest phone card is 15.70.

PARCHA: But I've got nothing!

BARTENDER: 15.70.

PARCHA: I only need one credit, woman. Just enough to shout: 'Get me the fuck out of here!'

BARTENDER: Mr Wiesiu!!! Come, please!

PARCHA: LET ME CALL! FUCK! ONE PHONE CALL! ONE PHONE CALL! IT'S ONLY EIGHTY GROSZY!

BARTENDER: Yes, it's only eighty groszy, but the cheapest card is 15.70. I don't care if you're a Romanian beggar or a celebrity Pope, that's how much the card costs. And I won't have any old fruitcake from the funny farm coming in here and making a phone call to wherever. I said that, right, Halina? And then Wiesiek arrived.

WIESIEK: How can I help? Is there a problem? What's the problem?

BARTENDER: Let me introduce you. This is Father Grzegorz. With his wife the nun. And their foetus the altar boy. Ha ha.

WIESIEK: How can I help?

PARCHA: Mr Wiesiek, hello there. The problem is this: I need to make a phone call and the ladies don't mind, but they say that I need to ask you...

WIESIEK: Do you have to scream blue bloody murder?

PARCHA: Of course not, but...

WIESIEK: Do you have to scream blue murder?

BARTENDER: Don't listen to him, he's been telling us stories, how he's some rich actor from Warsaw, but he can't buy himself the cheapest phone card 'cause he's got no money. They're some kind of junkies. But I know his mug from somewhere. That's it! You're that joker who steals the eggs from my henhouse.

PARCHA: No, that's not me! I... I curse you! A curse on you! A curse! A fucking curse! I hope your microwave blows up and blasts you all to hell.


## SCENE 3

PARCHA: This is worse than Romania. A bad dream; a bad dream that isn't a dream. This is poetry. I'm speaking poetry.

DŻINA: Getting back to my boy, I'm sure Mum would have picked him up from nursery. When was it? Wait, it was the day before yesterday. Thursday. I walked him to nursery. I remember it clearly, because he was screaming at the top of his voice, whaaaaa whaaaaa, like that. But did I pick him up? Did I say anything about picking him up?

PARCHA: Wait, let me focus, I'm trying to think about something else.

DŻINA: Try to remember, did I say anything?

PARCHA: I've no idea, sweetheart, I didn't know you on Thursday.

DŻINA: That's right, that's right, exactly. I think she must have picked him up because she always picks him up, because, for example, like now, I can't. You're right. That's what happened. He was standing there and screaming whaaaaa and she turned up. What do you think? That's what happened. Right? Unless she decided to take revenge on me by leaving him there.

PARCHA: Does he have house keys, just in case?

DŻINA: She does.

PARCHA: So he probably went home.

DŻINA: You think? (*Pause.*). He doesn't have keys, he's four years old, you moron.

PARCHA: Don't call me a moron, we're not at that level of intimacy. Fuck it I am a moron. Give away five thousand?! It's impossible, impossible. Five thousand, do you know how much money that is? People would eat their own shit for five thousand. For that money you could buy a house, with a field, and a fence, a fucking villa in Białystok.

DŻINA: Actually, I'm not even sure if I took him to nursery. He might have stayed at my mum's. He's probably still there playing Heroes or Lego by himself. He knows how to play by himself.

PARCHA: Stop talking bullshit, stop. The most important thing now is that I have to be on set at eight am tomorrow.

DŻINA: Back off, will you? I'm not calling her. Don't even try to persuade me, I'm not going to call her. Why should I? So she can throw a heap of shit at me? I know what she'll say. Yesterday I blew the child maintenance. She ain't gonna let that one drop. She'll force me to get a proper job. Assembling pens.

## SCENE 4

*Night, in a field, a WOMAN in her forties or fifties wearing smudged make-up stops the car, gets out, opens the boot, takes out a bottle of vodka and drinks from it. In the meantime, two poor Romanians run towards her car; losing their shoes as they go, they throw themselves onto the hood.*

PARCHA: (*Crying.*) A Warsaw number plate... Are you going to Warsaw?

WOMAN DRIVER: Thoo Warsawy.

PARCHA: You miracle, you supreme being, you're here. I called and you've come. Swear that you're not a mirage! It's a miracle. Miracles happen. To Warsaw, how many kilometres is that?

WOMAN DRIVER: Wha?

PARCHA: To Warsaw, how many kilometres?

WOMAN DRIVER: Hundud.

PARCHA: A hundred!! A hundred!! I told you. A hundred kilometres is a stone's throw. We're rescued! Resurrected! Mrs Professor. Mrs Queen. You're beautiful. We're coming with you! We're coming with you! How warm it is in here! How nice! We're normal people! We just look like this. Please. We'll behave ourselves. We won't fart!

WOMAN DRIVER: Welcm. You fell from the schky. Thisch ish not my car. Thisch ish a Vectra. You pressch here and here and here we goesch.

PARCHA: And my associate, she can come too, if she has to?

WOMAN DRIVER: Whaddo I care?

PARCHA: Let's go Dżina, the lady said if you have to, you can come too. I did the deal. I vouched for you. She DOESN'T STINK. She just looks like that.

*They're driving.*

How's it going? How's life? The weather, as we can see, is so-so; the cabbage crop failure this year was simply terrible...

*Silence*

WOMAN DRIVER: Of coursch. The wedder. Pressure. Lubberly.

*Silence*

PARCHA: And you're a driving with such flair, madam, but if you don't mind me asking... Could you drive a little straighter??

WOMAN DRIVER: Whateffer... It schimple, if schomething coming towards uscsh, z'tell me. I took out my lengisch and put somewhere overrear, but I can schee more or lessch. Schoo what where you're growing? Schtudents, are you schtudents, what do you schtudy? Doan be schcared, I'm not drung, doan be schcared, I can d-drive.

PARCHA: We're not students. We're Polish-speaking Romanians, we're lesbians, queers, Jews, we work in an advertising agency. Like I said before, we're going to Israel to plant trees and these inbred fucks out here won't give us a lift, not even to the end of the road. I'm Father Grzegorz from *Plebania* a very popular TV soap. I have to be on set at eight, so I have to get some sleep if I'm going to look good, take a shower, have a shave...

WOMAN DRIVER: Do you have a drive licence, by any schance?

PARCHA: No, not any more. Aaaa! Maybe she's got one, but I doubt it. Watch out!...Shit, what the fuck are you doing?

WOMAN DRIVER: If you doan haff one what the fuck are you doon in my car? Why do you thing I let you in? Schit.

Hey, cool cool, doan worry, we'll just keep drivering the way we are. The Lawwwd giveth, and the Lawwwd taketheth away... Or I'll teach you, thisch isch a clutch, thisch isch a gears and off you go. Or not. I'll drive myself... Thees is a car, thees is wheels, thees is all on credit... Cool cooooool, everythi und contrr. Fuck, I tell you, I'll tell you that, I tell you. You are so lucky, you youngstuz, thees car cost fif-ti thousand, for five-ti thousand you don't get just any old crap.

DŻINA: Excuse me, just a quick question, you got any snacks?

WOMAN DRIVER: F-fuck, Hungary, Turghee, Romanya, I know, a verrrrry beautiful country. Evbody saysch, Romania a mess, schhhit, faeces, Islam, chillren eading schit from the pavement. Thisch Cincinatti dischtator isch in scharge, peeble are are eading rubble, but thees is a grrrreat country with pepper, and frud, and holidaysss, and I there, we go ess-ski-ing with my husand there. Sooo great. You're travllin. You have no things, no lug-jij, credit cards, monii, you're just travllin. Free from all the constant eating and schitting of the world. You have no idea what a messch it all isch.

DŻINA: You know, sometimes we find something in a bin, people throw away such good stuff nowadays, whole chickens, hot dogs. Sometimes when I take the rubbish out, you know, when I'm throwing it out, something tells me not to let go of the bag...

WOMAN DRIVER: Schure, fer-oh it out, bins-sra great thing, ones I even found a lampshade, Art Nerver, everyone arks about it.

*Silence*

DŻINA: That's all very well but I need a piss.

WOMAN DRIVER: Wha? You cun pee where you wann. Theesees my husband's Vectra, high doan keh, it makes me happy. Adieu.

*Pause. The WOMAN DRIVER is zigzagging more and more with her driving, the Romanians are getting frightened.*

PARCHA: Countess, you you you... You know, you're a great driver and the conversation is delightful, but but let's stop for some coffee. How about it?

WOMAN DRIVER: Wha? Now look sunschine, doan tll me, what do do because I is tooking you with me ohnee because I'm thing thaat you got a drive licence. Sooo no complains.

*They continue zigzagging.*

PARCHA: Because, after all, the coal barge The Ibuprofen, the one that's taking us to a number of places, Israel among them, is setting off soon... I'm on set tomorrow at eight and you're taking the roundabout route zigzagging like that. We'd rather live you know... My associate here left her child in nursery a few days back. He's probably still there, playing with his Lego.

DŻINA: Why remind me about that, arsehole? So I have to think about it all over again?

PARCHA: He's sitting there. Without a bedtime story, without his jim-jams, in his three day old pants, in his own shit and piss. But the cavalry is coming. If we don't get back soon, her mother'll ground her for weeks.

DŻINA: Arsehole, stupid fuck.

WOMAN DRIVER: Wow, how educadid, leesten to her, no sur-pie-sis ere, is troo that I myself fee a lill fucked up and I admit that, yes, I got fucked up, but there is no poin in getting out now, because thees is why-uld Polish wildissniss here, this is a swamp. Theh weell bee some point where it makes sense, schum petrol stayschun, schum peeple, then you can ged oud but I doan have the heart to leaf you wee-er.

*She takes a bottle from beneath her legs and drinks, she goes to pass it on.*

Bottoms up!

PARCHA: You're doing my head in, woman! Keep it together! What the fuck is going on – bottoms up?! Just fucking focus, will you, my nerves are shot, me, an old Romanian who's been around the block a bit. Where are we, after all? In Białowieska Forest ? Stop the car. I said: stop.

*WOMAN DRIVER brings the car to a screeching halt, it's in the middle of a forest, no light to be seen, no sound to be heard.*

WOMAN DRIVER: Reekwescht schtop. You schudda sayd so before. Heeere you goes. Welcm to the woods. Hey, tomorrow or whenever... schend me texx if yoo fine enny muschoomsch.

Ha, ha, ha.

*They continue driving; the WOMAN DRIVER is drinking straight from the bottle.*

Wayd a minnit because it's ringering.

*She picks up the phone.*

Yesch. Yesch. Yesch. And whad elss and whad elss. No, I'm not drunk. I'm drivering. With my frenns if you musst know, whoss your namesch, you two?

PARCHA: Laszlo Cesspool. And she's Regina. Surname: Magdelina.

WOMAN DRIVER: (*To the phone.*) Regina and Something, my frenns. No, I'm not crazy. Reelly simply nysch, oben yun peeple, nysch, no, I'm not drunk, not at all. You'ff been wayding for me three hoursch? No, I'm not drunk. And who's tor-ging there in the bagroun? No-un? Is it her? You don't need to pretend, just some gurrrl schtopped by to play on the computer and youse on the ph-phone for howse and she's getting bored, sad and naykd and she's getting cold, goat her, lick her cunt. No, I'm not drunk, I'm not, or maybe I am, so what if I am? I don't know wheh I am, tell the troof, because there are none of those signspots. There's sum soarra cunnrysigh, woods aggshulley, branches and berries, maybe is Norway? I'll get there soon, so geddonwiddit, then you can make me schum dinner. Dee-nuh. Yes, you burn it and then add a little too musch salt. So it's burnt. And too salty. Thaz the way I like it. Because if I don't crash your fucking car then I'll ged bag very hunrey. Bye. Adieu.

PARCHA: Did you hear that, Dżina? We'll be there soon. It's not far. I'll make it to the set. Let me borrow the phone, I need to make a call.

WOMAN DRIVER: Geh your fiffy han offa mi. Sorry for my husband. He's triff-eyed I'm gonna craaaaaash his fucking car. I unnerstand him so well. Now his loversch pissched off widdim, it was schuppose to be a romannic evenin, she dunned her homework schtraight arffer school, changed her nappy and came right over, you know w-whad I mean, it's true love, he has her under Mariusz in his m-mobile. And now he's payzin angreely up and down from window to window with his limp dick, telling her: 'Wayd for me, darhlink, I haffoo cut my nails' and other sorry excuses, sssso he can stand by the window shitting his pants that

50

his Vectra will arrive one wheel, then another and the ress of it in a fucking body bag.

Ha ha ha.

AAAAAAAAAA!!!!!!!!!!!

*There is an accident, the car crashes into something in the darkness.*

*The WOMAN DRIVER lies bleeding on an airbag, the Romanians are all okay; there's a wild boar lying in front of the car.*

PARCHA: (*Outraged.*) What the fuck was that? What is it?

WOMAN DRIVER: (*Losing consciousness.*) A hedge...hog...

PARCHA: Hedgehog...Hedgehog! I'll give you hedgehog!

Hey, Countess. Hey, wake up. Hey you... I think she kicked the bucket. She's really screwed us, out in the open, in the middle of fucking nowhere, she can't be serious.

DŻINA: So give her first aid.

PARCHA: Me? You think it's that easy? I don't have time, I'm in a hurry. She'll be fine, right?

DŻINA: How do you know?

PARCHA: Is she alive? Yes she is. Life is the basis of everything. She'll be fine, she's got charisma, see for yourself. She's got this little moustache. The kidder.

DŻINA: Maybe you're right, there's no point. So what do we do?

PARCHA: See her phone anywhere? I have to call and let them know I might be late on set.

DŻINA: It's fucked itself up

PARCHA: What do you mean?! That's unreal.

*He throws the crushed phone away, looks beneath her legs, takes out the WOMAN DRIVER's bottle and drinks greedily.*

Do you want a swig? There's a drop left. I can't get totally trashed.

Come on, let's take her watch at least. That's a lovely watch you have there, dear, Seiko, those diamonds are the height of fashion. Don't bear a grudge, I'm a desperate man. Twelve-fifteen. That's impossible! She must have the wrong time zone. I guess it must be about eleven, there's still a chance I'll make it.

*He puts on the watch; reaches for the WOMAN DRIVER's bag.*

A-ha, she's got a bag. Maybe some cash. I've got to buy a phone card. No, you do it, it's too disgusting. I've never done anything wrong in my life. Except for some minor misdemeanours back in nursery school. Second thoughts, give it back. I'll do the checking. You're not to be trusted. You're crazy and a drug addict.

Chewing gum – we'll take that and share it. Contraceptive pills – that's disgusting – you want them?

DŻINA: Get them away from me.

PARCHA: Go on, take them. They can give you one hell of a hallucination.

DŻINA: Leave me alone, you Neanderthal. Take them yourself: we definitely need to wipe out your gene pool.

PARCHA: Go on, take them. You need them. Nooo, okay, I was joking, this old tart's eaten half of them anyway. Such a drunken old hag and still mating, the beast. Oh la la. That's fucking gross.

DŻINA: Will you shut up, I can't listen to you, you retard. Fuck, put the bag back. What if she's dead and that's a corpse? You can't steam a stiff.

PARCHA: What, you think she doesn't fuck? Maybe she takes it for acne? Right? Calm down. Warpaint, crayons, eye-shadow, fingerpaints. I'll take that for you. You need it, believe me... You don't know how bad you look but it's staring me in the face. If you don't want it, I'll give it to someone else. Wait, maybe she's got another phone. There's a purse. She's got thirty zlotys. THIRTY ZLOTYS! We really hit the jackpot! When we get to a garage, we'll buy you some WET WIPES.

(*To the* WOMAN DRIVER.) You slapper. You blew it all on drink. That'll teach you.

## SCENE 5

*In a ditch. They get out of the car, they limp on through total darkness.*

PARCHA: No mother, no father, the two of us alone, together at last, to the end. I'll go mad. A drunken old slag gives us a lift and drives straight into a wild boar. A wild boar from the forest, don't forget. It could've attacked us. People aren't normal, she could've killed us. People are hopeless. I have to make a phone call, or there'll be a scandal.

DŻINA: Shut up, shut up, shut up. That's all I ask.

PARCHA: Okay, okay, shut up yourself. I hate you. I always hate girls I fuck when I don't love them. It is disgusting, disgusting, sex without love, it's just porn. In out, out in.

DŻINA: W-what? What did you say? I didn't fuck you, I've already told you. We didn't fuck.

PARCHA: How can I trust you, how can I trust you, what reasons do I have to trust you? Woman, you've got total amnesia for all I know. Now you remember, now you don't. God giveth and God taketh away, how'd you know if you slept with me or not, when I don't even know? Please, don't make me laugh. I suspect that I slept with you, because I feel like shit and it was probably because of that, precisely because of that, I slept with you. I hate mechanical, industrial, perfunctory sex with unknown women who I can't even be arsed to look down on, with whom I feel a terrifying void and emptiness, an alien body beneath my hands, which might as well belong to an animal, an alien body with no face, choo-choo, and when it's all over you lie there. Breathing. Your breath like the sound of cars driving by, like a siren passing, like a shadow falling. It's hilarious. Spit and sperm dry up like the rain. Because these are the juices of love, the juices of love. Spit! Sperm! Egg white! And flour and water paste.

DŻINA: I didn't fuck you, no way, no way! I told you, it never happened.

PARCHA: Yes you did! You took advantage of me when I was unconscious and defenceless!

*They walk in silence.*

(*Unable to restrain himself.*) You're a perfect mother, no two ways about it. You walked out on your kid just like that, don't say a word, I'd rather not think about it. Fucking kid in nursery all alone day and night. Even the cleaning ladies have gone, the caretaker's gone and he's sitting there in a puddle of piss and he's playing with these cars, because what else is he to do, what else is there? Even the toys are laughing at him. Okay, Okay. Easy now, just messing about, let me know if I push it too far.

*Pause, they walk, there are no cars around.*

I'm sorry. I have to keep on talking or we'll fall asleep. And freeze. I'm cold. I'm going mad from the cold. How did they survive these places back in the day?

DŻINA: So lie down.

PARCHA: Very funny. Very funny.

DŻINA: Don't you think I'm cold too? Cold as a cold cunt.

PARCHA: So what? You want me to give up my jacket now? No way. I'd be dead in fifteen minutes. Though I'd probably get eternal life. You could take part in my beatification.

*Pause.*

So you think we're going to die? Now? Like, right away?

DŻINA: Yes.

*Pause.*

PARCHA: What hopelessness, what a come down.

Something's been telling me to say no to drugs, to stop doing this shit. You junkies, for you it's everyday life, but for normal people it's really destructive. Then someone tells me there's a fancy dress party called 'Rats, Scabs and Scroungers', 'Eve invites you to Mokotów...' I dress up, make an effort, colour my teeth with a marker, put on some stinky rags, the cab driver doesn't even want to take me. I arrive, meet this chick, that's you, it's supposed to be fun. We're dancing, I'm offered some concoction and then BAM! Romania! I'm a Romanian! I'm going somewhere, I give away my money! Me, Father Grzegorz, a respectable bachelor. You talked me into it. Why did you have to remind me? Now I'm pissed off and it's all coming back to me. Late on set: yes. Die: yes. But not like this. This is madness.

To be honest, I'm scared, deep down in my subconscious I fear that I might not in fact be rewarded with eternal life. Only God knows – in theory at least – if I was better or worse at certain times. But the Catholic Church will fucking harass me with its dogmas, confessions and fasts. It will fuck me over big time. Me. It will fuck Father Grzegorz.

DŻINA: God, you exist, I see a light.

PARCHA: Impossible. It's not possible.

DŻINA: It might be a house.

PARCHA: A house! We're saved! Warmth! A pot of tea, not to mention food! Clean sheets! I'll call Warsaw...sure I'll be a little late, but I'll be there. Father Grzegorz. On top form, as always.

*End of Act Two.*

# Act Three

## SCENE 1

*PARCHA and DŻINA stand at the door of a house without a fence, in the open, they pound on the door really hard. They call out:*

PARCHA / DŻINA: Help! Help! Hello! Save us! Open the fucking door!

*Finally some noises are heard, numerous locks, clasps, latches and then more of the same are opened up. The unshaven head of an OLD MAN appears.*

OLD MAN: Is that you?

PARCHA: Yeah, it's us. In real life.

OLD MAN: Are you alone?

PARCHA: Of course we're alone.

OLD MAN: (*Releases the chain.*) Are you sure?

DŻINA: Yeah, we're sure.

OLD MAN: Come in, but hurry.

*Inside the OLD MAN's house. He collects rubbish, the interior is a mess, there are things piled everywhere, two bathtubs, shoes, all the garbage of the world; the TV is on.*

(*Watching them.*) Father Grzegorz? That's right, isn't it! Father Grzegorz!

PARCHA: Yes, that's me, I'm the actor who plays him...

OLD MAN: What an unexpected-unprecedented visit. A night-moonlight! Father Grzegorz! At last-finally the good Father has come to visit me. What an honour-pleasure. And this woman-girl, who's she?

PARCHA: My associate-acquaintance.

OLD MAN: Angel?

PARCHA: That's right. She's an ex-prostitute drug addict, you know, my son. I took it upon myself to give her shelter.

OLD MAN: But where's your cassock?

PARCHA: What cassock?

OLD MAN: Cold-nippy in a cassock, right? The wind blows right through and freezes your nuts off. So you came in normal dress?

PARCHA: Give it a rest, old man. I'm blushing. You got anything to eat, Grandad? Something hot to drink? My arse is frozen to the bone. My associate's as well.

OLD MAN: Not really, not really, no. I was hoping-expecting you might help me, Father, help me to do my shopping. I can't leave the house.

PARCHA: Why? What do you mean?

OLD MAN: Don't ask, Father – you don't want to know-no. As soon as I go out, they come in. I step outside and I hear woosh, woosh and I know they're coming. They come in they turn the locks and they touch, touch. They come in and touch me. Right here, you see, Father? I can't go out, because I have to come straight back in.

PARCHA: You got a phone, Grandad?

OLD MAN: I don't have a phone. I did have one. But they were always calling.

*He climbs onto the bed.*

Here are the marks. This is where they touch me. This is where they touch me. Here are marks where they touched me. They come in and touch me here. I can't go out even for just a minute, not even for one minute, because they come straight away, straight away. And they touch me.

PARCHA: Grrrreat.

DŻINA: Can we stay here for the night? We're really fucked. We've walked all the way from Kazakhstan-from Uzbekistan. We just want some kip, we won't bother you.

OLD MAN: Have forty winks – stay the night. It seems-appears... Father Grzegorz, always. But you must be careful. They don't sleep. You have to be on your guard. Perhaps when they see-notice that it's you, Father Grzegorz, maybe then they'll come to their senses.

## SCENE 2

*PARCHA and DŻINA are on the bed, covered with rugs, they look at the watch, chew gum, they are in a claustrophobic room filled with rubbish, with a gurgling bathroom. DŻINA is playing with some kind of string.*

PARCHA: Well? Well? Well?

You got what you wanted. Your party, your fucking 'extreme poverty' fancy dress party cost me five grand and my career. So let's party! We could play a word game.

DŻINA: A word game.

PARCHA: Don't repeat after me. I'm not going to make it now. They'll wait, they'll call, it'll be in all the papers. They'll kick my arse out the door, that's for sure and then they'll hire some useless fuck, tell the viewers that Father Grzegorz had to undergo plastic surgery after a fire! What a mess! I'm totally fucking screwed!

DŻINA: Screwed.

PARCHA: Where's my mobile? Where did I leave it? Maybe you jacked it? No. You should think about your kid. You left your kid at nursery, that's a real moral achievement! You should never have had him at all. What's his name? It's a boy, right?

*Silence*

Well, say something or I'll drop off. Then Grandad will come with an iron bar, he'll think that we came here to touch him and he'll beat our fucking brains out. I'll keep watch, but let me ask you this: why should I keep watch and not you? Why should I have to be the responsible one? Who the hell are you, anyway? What d'you do for a living?

DŻINA: I'm an artist of life.

PARCHA: Ooooo. Just as I thought. And anything apart from that?

DŽINA: I don't know. Not much really.

PARCHA: That's right.

DŽINA: I filled out invoices. Mum arranged it. But I had a hangover that day so it was all double, double rows and columns. And there were these other sluts sitting there in festering cardigans they'd crocheted themselves, just glaring at me. The kind of sad bitches who photocopied their tits after hours and compared results. Oh yeah and last summer, I worked this burger stand, frying sausages, chips, you know. In one square metre, me and a hundred and fifty litres of hot, three-year-old frying oil. Lady Greaseball. But I always jacked something, ten zlotys maybe, so in the evening I'd have these ten zlotys. TEN ZLOTYS. And I'd buy a beer in the bar, all proud of myself. And I'd be sat there with a face as red as tinned ham, Miss Keilbasa, oil dripping from my hair onto the table, and my mum would say: finally, finally, finally something. Finally.

PARCHA: That's really pleasant. You should do something worthwhile with your time, take up something or other. Unless you really have no talent whatsoever.

DŽINA: And so I go out, in out, out in, all the time, I fuck all these jerks like you, even though I don't want to. I only go with them to get a decent night's sleep, no one screaming blue murder when I wake up with a hangover. We're in this studio flat, seventeen square metres. It's no joke when you've got a hangover and someone's clanging some fucking kettle or pot above your head, when you're dying and your kid brings his little keyboard to your bed and starts banging out 'We are little Blueberries' or 'This Little Piggy'. And they all think I fuck them because I want the greatest sex of my life in seventeen different positions with no mercy, even if they've got a limp dick, they still have to try to put it in and get it out at least once because otherwise it doesn't count. And in the morning they go: Oh God, where are your clothes, you must be in a hurry, I know I am; You finished that tea yet? I can get you a thermos flask!

Ha ha ha. Ha ha ha. And I'm on my, I'm on the tram, ram-tam-tam. And I roll up the stairs, I open the door. Where were you?! Look! What do you think you're doing! This is your child!

Mum, Mum, who was the father of Copernicus?

Perhaps you should tell him who his father is, his father, well???

God, who else?

All day he played Heroes. And then he pissed himself. I'm sorry but I'm turning the vacuum on...

Mummy, why did this piggy go to market!!! Why did this piggy go to market!!! Why did this piggy have roast beef, and the other one have none!!!! And this little piggy go wee wee wee all the way home... Mummy! Mummy!

That actress on TV, she's been sleeping around too.

Listen how he learned to play the national anthem on his little piano! Listen! All the verses! And backwards as well! Go fetch your little piano and play it for Mummy. Not there, stupid.

Look at the state of you! Don't you have a home? Did you spend the night in a skip?

PARCHA: Well, I can't help you there, sweetheart. But it's an outrageous way to carry on. You should stop it, really, meet someone who won't treat you like a slut. Have you been tested for HIV? Well you should. Let's be serious, you have to find someone who might fall in love with you, or even if he doesn't, who'll stop you being a slut. Maybe you have some kind of subconscious complex based on a destructive relationship with your father.

DŻINA: God our father.

PARCHA: Me personally...

DŻINA: Would you lend me five hundred?

PARCHA: Me? To you?

DŻINA: My kid is really ugly. All the other women walk around with normal kids. Why do I have an ugly kid and not a normal one?

PARCHA: I hate casual sex with women who think of me as Father Grzegorz and that by fucking me they'll leave their mark on the world. I slept with Father Grzegorz, so I'm no longer a nobody...yadayadayada. I slept with Father Grzegorz. Girls, it was such a turn on. I thought I'd go insane.

DŻINA: I can't go back there. She'll fucking kill me.

PARCHA: I hate it. The worst thing is that they always succeed in luring me with their photo albums, stamp collections or range of herbal tea. Come on, this shelf is from Ikea, we have this here and we have that there, isn't it COOL?

DŻINA: I need a piss.

*She goes to the bathroom.*

PARCHA: We have this here and that there, and here we have some tits, don't peek, now. This here, that there. These are our tights, we throw them over there. And you, when you act, do you do more of this or of that, because I was wondering, and here, look at this scar, a terrible, terrible scar, well that's life! So here you go, look at this, this is that and that is this, and now I'll take a bath. And ooh, I'm back already, and everything's cool, right? So now what? You're going to sleep with your clothes on, are you crazy? Come on, let me show you where you'll be sleeping, and yes, that's where I'll be sleeping too, with you, can you believe it? Look... Me and you and you and me and I and Father Grzegorz, because you'd be wrong to think that I'm just some ordinary waitress who works at Café-Café, just some girl handing out free copies of the Metropol outside the university. It's absurd to think of me as ordinary, on the contrary, I must be extraordinary, because you're here now and I know you.

And I lie there like a burnt out whore in a burnt out ruin.

I'm wondering if I turned the iron off.

I'm wondering what trams go from here.

What fucking Romania is this? What loneliness.

Oh, you've already shot your load, well that's good, actually, I'm really happy. I'm going to sleep now. Oh look, I'm awake. Are you leaving so soon? But where are you going? The girls will be along in a minute to see you! They say that you're terrible to me, just terrible! A poor girl like me! And they say, that if only you could be a little more like this, like that!

And I go, I go by tram. No mummy. No daddy. Alone to the end of the line.

And now I'm fired from my fucking job... No, in three hours' time I'm fired from my fucking job. I'm a nobody. I'm finished.

*He stands at the bathroom door in a new attack of euphoria.*

Dżina! Dżina? Hey.

Now I know what your problem is. I just worked it out, simple really.

DŻINA: (*Trying to make a rope for herself.*) Yes?

PARCHA: Just don't take this the wrong way. There's no love in your life! Simple as that. Nobody loves you! Nobody loves you and that's why you're so unhappy when you screw these guys who don't love you, it's pointless, it's empty, it doesn't mean anything. Love is the most important thing in life. Someone who won't tell you to fuck off in the morning and, you know what, Dżina? Love will purify you.

Hey, hey what are you doing in there?

Are you taking a bath? What for?

Come out, I don't want to sit here on my own. I'm scared. You went off to the bathroom and just left me here.

I won't peek.

Why are you taking a bath?

I wouldn't fuck you anyway, not even if you washed in boiling water.

Dżina, hey!

I was only joking, you idiot.
Open the fucking door.
Open the door!

*He pulls at the doorknob, opens the door.*

*Inside DŻINA is hanging on a rope; she has hanged herself while he has been talking.*

What are you doing? Why did you do that?
How could you?!!! What is this? What is this? Get down from there.
AAAA!!!

DŻINA: So, I hanged myself.

PARCHA: So stay hanging there, I'm getting the hell out.

DŻINA: No, fuck you! You can't just leave me here by myself.

PARCHA: Don't even ask, I'm getting the fuck away from here.

*And what comes afterwards, and what I write would happen afterwards: PARCHA runs out, DŻINA cuts the rope with the penknife and runs after him; they push the terrified OLD MAN in his long johns on their way out:*

God bless you, we've got a boat to catch.

*The coal barge The Ibuprofen comes through the snow; they run onto its deck where they are warmly welcomed by the Romanian crew and passengers:*

CREW / PASSENGERS: At last! / Here you are! / We've been waiting for you...

*Finally, finally! They are handing out language school leaflets and candy wrappers and everybody is kissing their hands. An ecstatic party of benefit claimants. The participants eat branches and soil; they hold old, drooping balloons in their hands and they sing piercing Romanian songs. A WAITER says to PARCHA:*

WAITER: Mr Bułacze, it's an honour. Look, I've prepared a pepper stuffed with scraps of meat! Just for you and your wife. Would you like to try it?

63

PARCHA: Of course I would, but first I must wash my hands. I've been on the road all night.

*He goes into the bathroom and sees DŻINA hanging there.*

*The End.*